Ace the IELTS

IELTS General Module – How to Maximize Your Score

Third Edition

Simone Braverman

www.IELTS-Blog.com

Author Note

Correspondence concerning this book should be addressed to Simone Braverman
via e-mail simone@ielts-blog.com

D1362409

Ace the IELTS
IELTS General Module – How to Maximize Your Score (Third Edition)
ISBN 978-0-9873009-8-0
© July 2015 by Simone Braverman

Limits of Liability/ Disclaimer of Warranty

The author and publisher of this book and the accompanying materials have used their best efforts in preparing this program. The author and publisher make no representation or warranties with respect to accuracy, applicability, fitness or completeness of this program. They disclaim any warranties (expressed or implied), merchantability or fitness for any particular purpose. The author and the publisher shall in no event be held liable for any loss or other damages, including but not limited to special, incidental, consequential or other damages. As always, advice of competent professionals should be sought.

This manual contains material protected under International Copyright Laws and Treaties. Any unauthorized reprint or use of this material is prohibited.

From the author

I am very grateful for all the help and support I've received from all the members of my team, namely:

Vladimir Levitin – for great research
Roman Itskovich and Gregory Braverman – most talented Internet gurus
Nataly Dehter-Vaksman - for excellent legal advice
Eduard and Dina Somin – for superb ideas

Together there is no mountain we can't climb!

Acknowledgements

Thanks to the many authors, organizations and websites that have so kindly permitted us to use their material in our test, or allowed us to use the material under a creative commons license / public domain.

Endangered Sharks in Australia - http://www.environment.gov.au, http://www.supportoursharks.com
Flexible Working in our Workplace - http://www.acas.org/
A Threatened Breed (Polar Bears) - http://www.wwf.org.uk/

Table of Contents

What this book is about

This guide is here to teach you the IELTS test, not the English language. Why?
Even if English is your first language, you can forget about getting a good score in IELTS, unless you are prepared. Three main problems will get in your way: *time, tricks and logical traps*.

When it comes to IELTS, **time is your worst enemy**. You need to do things fast. Of course you would get all the answers right if you had the time. But the reality is that there are a lot of questions to be answered, a lot of writing to be done, and very little time to do it.

This guide teaches you **HOW TO**:

- Listen, hear the right answers and write them down FAST

- Scan through the text and deal with all kinds of questions FAST

- Get your essay written FAST

- Build a speech in your head on any topic FAST

- Know and avoid the traps when you see them

This book might not make your English perfect, but it will certainly help you to get in shape and Ace the IELTS!

Attitude tips

In my opinion (which was validated by the IELTS scores of the people I trained) you don't need more than 4 weeks of daily training. Set aside 3 hours that you devote to practice for IELTS – and it will get you the desired result.

I believe that if you can read and understand this book, your English is good enough. Just stick to the guidelines of this book and they will help you get the best IELTS score you can with your current level of English. You can even give yourself a *day off* once a week, and still be able to ace the IELTS!

To receive free IELTS advice and updates to your email go to http://www.ielts-blog.com and subscribe. You will be pleasantly surprised by the amount of useful information and friendly support you will receive.

How to use this book

The way this manual has been put together makes it possible for you to read the main chapters (Listening, Reading, Writing or Speaking tips) in **any** order you like - each is completely independent of the other. You don't have to follow the order in which the book is written.

If you don't have much time, I suggest reading this book and doing only the exercises that are included in it, no extra work. This is not the ideal way though.

In case you do have the time, I highly recommend that you read and pay attention to all the tips in this manual and then try to use them when you practice real IELTS tests.
There are links to IELTS materials at the end of every main chapter and a detailed study plan at the end of the book.

At the end of the book there are Pocket tips – short summaries of the most important hints in each of the chapters - Listening, Reading, Writing or Speaking. Every time you practice, read them before you start a test – they will refresh your memory and focus you on what's really important.

Enjoy!

The IELTS Routine

The IELTS test consists of four parts:

Listening, Reading, Writing and Speaking.

Listening takes about 40 minutes - 30 minutes to listen to a recording and to answer questions on what you hear, and 10 minutes to transfer your answers to the Answer Sheet.

Reading takes 1 hour and your task is to read passages of text and to answer questions according to what you have read. There are also other types of assignment which I will cover later on.

Writing also takes 1 hour and is divided into 2 sub-parts: 20 minutes to write a letter and 40 minutes to write an essay.

Speaking takes up to 15 minutes and consists of 3 parts: a Personal Interview, a Short Speech and a Discussion.

All the parts continue one after another, and only before the Speaking do you get a little break. In some cases the Speaking section is held on a different day.

The Listening test at a glance

Listening consists of 4 sections. There are 40 questions in total. You need to answer all the questions as you listen to the recording. The recording is not paused at any time and you hear it only once. The questions get more difficult as you progress through the test.

Are you scared yet? Don't be! There is a technique to get you through it. Just make sure that your answers are readable and easy to understand when you copy them to the Answer Sheet. You may write in **pencil only**.

The Reading test at a glance

The Reading test consists of about 4 text passages and has 40 questions in total. Your job is to read the passages and either answer questions, label diagrams, complete sentences or fill gaps. For every type of task there are instructions and an example. Passages are taken from books, newspapers, magazines and the topics are very diverse, from scuba diving to space exploration. Passages progress in difficulty, with the first being the easiest and the fourth is the hardest.

The good news is that you don't really have to read the whole passage, thanks to techniques that I will refer to later. The not-so-good news is that there is no additional time to copy your answers to the Answer Sheet and you need to squeeze it into the 60 minutes that you have. Please, don't forget to do this – I witnessed someone who did forget, and it was not a pretty sight. The poor guy was crying, he received a score of 0 for the **whole** Reading test. Here too you may write **in pencil only**, no pens are allowed.

The Writing test at a glance

Writing has 2 sub-tasks. The first one is to write a letter based on a scenario you receive, using about 150 words. The second task is to write an **essay** on a given topic, to present and justify an opinion or give a solution to a problem, using no fewer than 250 words.

Nothing to worry about here! Once you start using certain structures which I'll explain later on for the letter and the essay, in addition to your imagination, it is a piece of cake. This task requires a bit of training, but after you have written a few essays and letters you will be well-prepared for the test and you will feel **confident**.

The Speaking test at a glance

This is the fun part of the test, for many reasons. You get to rest before it. You are a little tired from the previous 3 parts and therefore more relaxed. The examiners are trained to smile no matter what, so you feel as if you are speaking to your best friend.

The first sub-part of the Speaking test is an interview, which means that the examiner asks you questions about yourself, your work, studies, parents, brothers/sisters, pets, etc. This is an easy task to prepare for.

In the second sub-part of the Speaking test you receive a card with 3-4 questions. After one minute, during which you have to think about something to say, you should give a short speech for one to two minutes, which answers those questions. At the end the examiner might ask you a couple of additional questions.

In the third sub-part of the test you have a discussion with the examiner. The topic is somehow related to the one from section two, but it is about more abstract ideas. You have to express and justify your opinions.

The examiner will record your session. Don't worry about it; the recording is to test the examiner and not you.

Tips for the Listening Test

In general

The Listening Test is probably the one people get most scared of. To help yourself overcome that fear, start watching TV programs in English. These are better than radio or audio books, because you also see images that help you understand the words you hear.

Listening – a skill, not a gift!

From my experience, in many cases listening is the least developed skill. So if you feel especially weak in that area, pay attention to the following tips, as they will help you improve your Listening ability. Remember – nobody is born with it, it's just a skill and you learn it. If you think your listening needs no improvements – skip the "Teach yourself the words" part, move forward to the tips which follow that part.

Teach yourself the words

The only way to improve your Listening ability is to train your ears to separate and understand the words you hear in the flow of a sentence. Often what you hear is a "Blablablablabla", which you can't break into words, and for that reason it makes no sense to you. When training, make a recording of the news, a lecture, a television program, a movie or an actual IELTS Listening test and work with it. I suggest using an MP3 player. You can easily record English from the radio or any other source onto it. It is also easy to repeat (re-play) sentences you didn't understand. An MP3 player is small and light, so you can use it in any spare moment that you have – riding on a bus or on a tram, walking the dog, taking a walk, etc.

First, listen, remember what you heard and stop the recording after each phrase. Even if you didn't understand the phrase, play it in your head a couple of times, like a broken record – "Tonight we have a special guest", "Tonight we have a special guest", "Tonight we have a special guest".

Then say it out loud. If you understood that phrase at first, this exercise will improve your pronunciation. If you didn't understand the phrase the first time, this repetition will give you more time to hear it better, break it into words and make sense out of them. If it is still difficult, you can always rewind and hear the phrase again.

There is a big difference between **seeing** a word printed on paper while reading, and **hearing** it. If you saw a word, it doesn't mean you will recognize it when you hear it.
This is why you must hear every word you have seen at least once.

Instructions will keep you safe

Every task in the IELTS Listening test has its instructions. It may sound stupid, but you really need to read them carefully. Why? Because they will tell you exactly what to do with the information: how many words you can use to answer questions, whether or not there is a table you must fill in, whether there is a list to choose words from, how many items you must name, etc. Remember, too, that if the answer must be in 3 words – write EXACTLY 3 WORDS, because writing four or two words will get you 0 score.

To make my point crystal clear, let's take the following scenario as an example:
The speaker on a recording says:
 "Well, if you are dieting, try to avoid fruits with lots of fructose like watermelon, mango, peaches or grapes."

The question in the booklet is:
"Name 2 fruits a person on a diet should not eat".

The answer may be "watermelon, mango" or "mango, peaches" or any combination of **two** items, but **never three or four**!!! Anyone who writes "watermelon, mango, peaches, grapes", just to be on the safe side, receives a score of zero for that question.

Note: when counting words - "a", "the" or a number (e.g. 159) is considered a word.

When instructions say "a maximum of 3 words" or "no more than 3 words" - you can write one, two or three words, but **never** more than three.

Divide and conquer!

The recording divides questions into **groups,** so for every grouping you are instructed to answer a group of 4-5 questions. There are 20-30 seconds of silence before each group.

The first thing you should do when the recording starts playing, is understand which group of questions you need to answer.

For example, the recording says: "Look at questions one to four". It means that you have about 20 seconds to look at those questions. Go over the questions, read them and underline keywords. Keywords are the words that contain the main idea of the question. They will help you guess what you will hear – numbers, opening hours, names, locations, etc.

Draw a line under the fourth question, so you won't look further before it's time to do so.

Next you will hear a piece of spoken language and answer the questions one to four **as you listen.** It means that you should be able to write one answer and listen to another.

After that, the recording will say the numbers of the questions in the next group. Repeat the same process, including drawing the line. This dividing technique is very efficient because every time you concentrate on a **limited** number of questions, it makes you more focused and in control.

Distractions

Don't get confused by all the different voices you are going to hear. The recording uses several different voices – of younger and older people, men and women. You may also hear different accents - Australian, British, American, Japanese, etc. The background noises also vary. It can be from an airport, a coffee-shop, a street, a university lecture hall, you name it. Be ready for it and don't let it distract you – because that is exactly what they want. Ignore the noises and listen for the answers.

Listen for specifics

When you are listening, look for descriptions and details, such as dates, places, telephone numbers, opening hours, years (1995), transportation (car, bike, train), etc.
If you hear them, but don't know where to place them yet – write them in the margins of the Listening booklet. Later you will have some time to check your answers. Going over the questions that you couldn't answer during the Listening passage, you might see if what you've written on the margins fits.

Answer as you listen

The reason you have to "answer as you listen" is that you immediately forget the sentences after you have heard them – because of stress, foreign language, constant flow of information, etc. After hearing the third sentence you won't be able to repeat the first. It means that when any part of the Listening is over you won't be able to remember any of the answers. So write them as you hear them, leave nothing for later.

Keep moving forward

A worst case scenario is you "losing the sequence of answers" – so you miss one answer and then you miss another one and so on. To prevent that from happening, always look one or two questions ahead. It sounds confusing, but after a little practice it becomes very natural and helps a lot. Even if you have missed the answer to a question – **admit it** and move to the next one, otherwise you will lose it too.

Know your clues

The answer is usually pronounced **louder and clearer**, so it is easier to hear and understand. If you can't hear something clearly (because the speaker swallows words or whispers), then probably the answer is not there. With some practice you will be able to tell the difference.

A good clue to an answer is when you hear a repetition of a word, a word being **spelled** out (G A R F U N K E L) or a number **dictated**.

Spelling tasks

As simple as it sounds, the spelling task is not so easy. You should practice a little to be prepared for it. Just ask someone to spell the names of cities from the following list for you. If you study alone, you could record yourself spelling those names and numbers, and then play it. The same goes for the list of telephone numbers I've included here. It is good practice and will only add to your confidence. Note: in numbers, "00" is sometimes read as "double o" instead of "zero-zero".

Cities	Numbers
Antananarivo	423-5207-0074
Brazzaville	628-2087-2311
Conakry	5167-832-0155
Gaborone	8746-221-0302
Johannesburg	5337-298-0132
Kinshasa	5900-231-7621
Libreville	4348-663-980
Lilongwe	11-267-55410
Mogadishu	101-9020-7624
Ouagadougou	413-2567-9011

Typical Listening tasks

Do you remember my promise – no surprises in IELTS? The following table shows you every type of task you may see in the Listening test booklet. Different task types come with different instructions, so if you see and remember them now, it will save you time later.
Of course, you won't get every type I show here in your test and the table looks a bit boring.
Anyway, my advice is to get to know them **now**.
Don't let them catch you off-guard!

Task Type	What you should do	Instructions in the booklet
Selecting pictures	From 3-4 pictures choose a picture that best describes what you hear.	Write the correct letter.
Multiple choice questions	There is a question and a number of answers (three, four or five), your job is to pick the right one (sometimes more than just one).	Choose the correct letter /Choose the correct answer.
Matching information	There is a list of items mentioned on the recording, for each item you should choose the correct option from another list in the booklet.	Write the correct letters next to questions.
Short-answer questions	Answer in 1, 2 or 3 words, as the instructions say.	Complete the notes/table. Use NO MORE THAN 3 WORDS for each answer.
Sentence completion	Complete sentences according to what you hear.	Complete the sentences below. Use NO MORE THAN 3 WORDS for each answer.
Form/Notes completion	A form/set of notes is given and you need to fill in blank fields.	Complete the form/notes. Write NO MORE THAN 3 WORDS for each answer.
Chart/Table completion	A chart/table with some blank cells is given; your job is to fill them according to the passage you hear.	Complete the chart/table. Use NO MORE THAN 3 WORDS for each answer.
Gap-fill	There are several sentences with missing words. You should pick the correct word and write it in each gap. Choose from the list (if there is one), or from what you have heard.	Complete the summary below by writing NO MORE THAN 3 WORDS in the spaces provided.
Plan/Map/Diagram labeling	Choose the correct options from the list or write a description of 1, 2 or 3 words for different parts of a drawing according to what you hear.	Label the plan/map/diagram below. Choose the correct letters / write NO MORE THAN 3 WORDS in the boxes/spaces provided.

Note: in some cases instructions in the booklet will indicate a different word limit for your answer. For example: "Use NO MORE THAN 2 WORDS AND/OR A NUMBER for each answer".

Eliminate wrong answers

When you deal with multiple-choice questions, elimination is a good strategy.
Usually only one answer is correct, unless the instructions say something else.

This task can be approached in a similar way to True/False/Not Given questions that appear in the Reading test. In multiple choice questions consider each option and ask yourself whether it is true, false or not given according to the recording. Of course the one option that is true is the correct answer! Any other answer is obviously incorrect.

Keep in mind that there are cases when all the choices are correct or none of them is correct. Read the instruction carefully and you will know what to do in such cases.

Gap-fill strategy

Look at the words around the gap to understand what's missing, a noun (like boy, toy, truck), an adjective (little, pretty, shiny) or a verb (stands, looks, moves).

For instance, if you see a **Noun** before the blank ("The boy is___"), it means that it's an **Adjective** ("The boy is **small**") or it's a **Verb** ("The boy is **smiling**") that is missing.

Once you have picked a word, write it above the gap and then read the whole sentence to be sure that it makes sense.

A hint: you do not need to change the word you heard on the recording, it should fit in the gap without changing its form or tense. If you think you must change the word for it to fit in the gap, then this word is likely to be the wrong answer.

"Chameleon" questions

They might use different words with the same meaning to confuse you. It could be expressions or synonyms.

For example, the recording might say "Kathrin was angry with her friends because…" and the question in the booklet might be "Choose two reasons why Kathrin was furious at her friends". The two words "angry" and "furious" describe the same emotion, but you can miss the answers if you try to hear the exact same word on the recording as that in the question booklet.

Watch out for traps

Trap Number One – unexpected turn

You might hear a speaker starting to say one thing and then, suddenly, continuing to something completely different. This is a trap, so make sure you don't fall for it. The rule here is "The last word counts". For example, if the speaker says "I want to visit that gallery on Monday. No, wait, I've just remembered that it is closed on Monday, so I will go on Wednesday.", and the question is "When...?" – the correct answer here is Wednesday, and Monday is a trap.

Trap Number Two – generalizations

You might hear a speaker first give a list of things and then say them **all in one word**. For example: "Well, I like to swim, hike, and camp – to be involved in outdoor activities." If the question is "What kind of activities..." the correct answer is "outdoor" and not "swimming", "hiking" or "camping".

Check the grammar

If the answer you give is grammatically incorrect – it cannot be the right one. Checking the grammar of your answers will give you an idea whether your answer is correct or not, especially in tasks like:
- Gap-fill
- Sentence completion

Use your time wisely

During the test, you have a little time between Listening sections. Use it to check and complete your answers.

Copy answers smartly

After the 30 minutes or so of the Listening test, there are 10 additional minutes. During the test you have written all of the answers in the Listening test booklet. These 10 minutes are given you to copy your answers onto the Answer Sheet, and you should use them **smartly**.

The Answer Sheet has 2 sides, one for the Reading test and one for the Listening test, so make sure you are writing on the Listening side. I include here an example of an Answer Sheet so you can get familiar with it and use it for practicing.

First, copy all the answers from the booklet onto the Answer Sheet, and pay attention to the following guidelines (as simple as they sound – they are BIG time savers):

- For multiple-choice questions and picture selection - just copy the letter of the correct answer, don't circle it.

- For sentence completion – just copy your answer, not the whole sentence.

- For True/False/Not Given questions – just copy T, F or NG, whatever your choice is.

- For gap-fills – just copy the word you have chosen for the gap.

- For answers written in short (like prof. advice) – write the full version (professional advice).

- Check that all the answers are clear and understandable.

Now, if you missed some questions – it is a good time to guess.

Answer Sheet looks like this:

1		21	
2		22	
3		23	
4		24	
5		25	
6		26	
7		27	
8		28	
9		29	
10		30	
11		31	
12		32	
13		33	
14		34	
15		35	
16		36	
17		37	
18		38	
19		39	
20		40	

For those of you who wonder why all the answers have to consist of a maximum of 3 words – here is the answer: there is not enough space on the Answer Sheet for anything longer than that!

Practice, practice, practice!

I strongly recommend that you use all the tips while practicing. In order to practice you are going to need samples of the Listening test, which can be found on the following internet sites (good quality, free of charge):

http://ielts-blog.com/online-practice/ - choose course type (General/Academic), then click on a big square button that says "FREE"
http://www.ieltsgym.com/?id=FreeEnglishlessons - online exercises with answers
http://www.esl-lab.com/- for this one you will need a Real Audio Player
http://www.ieltsontrack.com/mini_test.php?module=1 - a test with a transcript

Play the Listening samples and start using the tips while searching for answers. This is the only way to really understand how these tips work. You may have to play the same Listening file more than once, to practice different techniques.

Tips for the Reading Test

Test structure

General Training reading in most cases consists of several smaller passages that are taken from advertisements, official documents, booklets, manuals and 2 or 3 larger texts taken from books, magazines or newspapers.

As in the Listening test, questions in the Reading test are arranged in groups. Instructions will tell you which group of questions belongs to which paragraph or portion of text. You may see the questions before or after the passage they belong to.

Manage your own time

As I said before, time is your greatest enemy. In the Listening test it was managed for you, but the Reading test is a different story. You need to manage it very carefully yourself.

When you receive the Reading booklet, first of all count how many passages there are. Let's say there are 4 passages in the booklet. You could divide the hour into 4 equal parts and spend 15 minutes on each passage, but this is not the smartest way. The **smartest** way is to spend 10 minutes on the first passage, 15 minutes on the second, 15 on the third, and 20 on the last one. Why? Because they progress in level of difficulty!

Write down the time when you should start and when you should finish working on each passage and stick to it. In each passage set aside 2 minutes to copy your answers to the Answer Sheet. For example, in the first paragraph you should use 8 minutes to actually answer the questions (writing the answers on the booklet pages) and 2 to copy your answers to the Answer Sheet.

If you didn't finish a passage in time, move to the next one anyway. And whatever you do, please do not forget about the Answer Sheet (remember the guy with the ZERO score?)

If you have some time left by the end of the Reading test, make sure that you didn't forget to answer any question. Check and double check your answers. It can give you a few "easy" points if you find mistakes before the examiner does.

Don't read – scan!

It sounds absurd that you don't need to read in a Reading test, right?
Anyway, it's true. The biggest mistake you could make is to start the test by reading the whole passage.

The best thing is to scan quickly through the text. Don't try to understand every word! Just go over it and get the idea of what each paragraph is about. Usually you don't need to read the whole paragraph – a couple of first sentences are enough.

Make a map

The text before you resembles a strange, new territory. It is so easy to get lost inside all these words! What you need is a map that will help you to orientate yourself. Every paragraph in the passage has its own main idea, which is different from all the other paragraphs. Write in the margins near the paragraph what its topic is, and its main idea. If writing takes too much time, underline the words in the paragraph that explain its main idea. Congratulations! You have just created a map that will later guide you through the search for answers.

Learn the rules

First, read the instructions and the example. They show you exactly what your answer should look like – is it a number or a name, how many words must you write, etc. The following points are important because they may affect your score.

1.   Style

When filling in the answers, **copy the example's style.** To demonstrate, look at the following table:

	USA	Canada	Sweden
Divorce rate	*Example 1*: **55%**		
Marriage	*Example 2*: **first**		

Example 1

If the example says "55%", give your answer in this exact form, a number and %. Any other form or style (like "55" or "55 percent" or "fifty five percent") may harm your score!

Example 2

If the example says "first", answering in any other form or style (like "1st", "1" or "first marriage") may harm your score.

2.   Word Limit

Usually if there is a word limit for an answer, it is no more than 3 words. Prepositions (in, of, to, at, etc), articles (a, an, the) and numbers (5, 12, etc) are considered words. The reason behind this 3 word limit is a small space on the Answer Sheet.

3.   One question - One answer

Don't give more than one answer to one question, even if you see more than one option. It will result in a ZERO score. For example, if you see names of 3 countries that qualify as an answer and the question asks to name just one – don't even think of giving 2 or 3 names, the only correct answer is to name exactly one. Only if they ask for two names, should you name two, etc.

Types of task

The kinds of task you may have to deal with are in the table below. Different task types come with different instructions. It is important for you to see them all now, so nothing will surprise you during your IELTS test. Understanding in advance what you need to do in every type of task gives you a huge advantage. This way, during the test, you will only read the instructions to confirm what you already know.

Task Type	What you should do	Instructions in the booklet
Matching headings	There is a list of headings, your job is to choose the most suitable heading for every paragraph of the text.	Choose the most suitable heading for each paragraph from the list of headings below.
Matching information	Your job is to find in which paragraph or section of the text some particular information is located.	Which part of the text mentions the following? Choose the correct letter.
Multiple choice questions	There is a question and a number of answers (three, four or five), your job is to pick the right one (sometimes more than just one).	Choose the correct letter.
Short-answer questions	Answer in 1, 2 or 3 words, as the instructions say.	Using NO MORE THAN THREE WORDS answer the following questions.
Sentence completion	Complete the sentences according to what you read. There may be a list of sentence endings to choose from, or you may be required to use words from the text to complete each sentence.	Complete the sentences below. Write the correct letter / Use NO MORE THAN THREE WORDS for each answer.
Chart/Table completion	A table with some blank cells is given; your job is to fill them according to the passage you read.	Complete the table/chart below using information from the reading passage. Use NO MORE THAN THREE WORDS for each answer.
True/False/Not Given task	There is a statement, which can be True, False or Not Given in the passage; you need to decide according to what you read.	Read the passage and look at the statements below. Write TRUE if the statement is true, FALSE if the statement is false and Not Given if the information is not given in the passage.
Yes/No/Not Given task	There are statements which can agree with the claims of the writer, contradict them or be unrelated to the writer's claims; you need to decide according to what you read.	Read the passage and look at the statements below. Write YES if the statement agrees with the claims of the writer, NO if the statement contradicts the claims of the writer and NOT GIVEN if it is impossible to say what the writer thinks about this.

Task Type	What you should do	Instructions in the booklet
Matching features	Match statements to a list of features from the text.	Choose the correct letter.
Gap-fill	There are several sentences with missing words, you should pick the correct word and put it in the gap. Choose from the list (if there is one), or from the text.	Complete the summary below. (Choose your answers from the box at the bottom of the page)
Diagram labeling	Write a description of 1,2 or 3 words for different parts of a drawing according to what you read.	Label the diagram below. Use NO MORE THAN THREE WORDS from the passage for each answer.

Go fishing!

Now it is time to start "fishing" for answers. Read the questions one-by-one, for every question see what its theme is. Then find it (or something close to it) on your map - that is the paragraph to search for the answer.

Choose your battles

If any question takes you too much time – give up, move to the next one. Don't forget to mark it with some sign (like "?"), so you can identify it and come back to it later. There are a lot of questions and you might miss the easy ones if the hard ones take all of your time. Another reason to leave hard questions until later is that after you do all the easy ones, you know more about the text, so then solving the tricky questions might become easier.

Use passage layout

Every text and every paragraph in it has a certain structure, meaning it is written according to some rules. Usually the first paragraph contains the main idea of the passage and the author's opinion. The last paragraph often summarizes the main points of the passage.

Every paragraph has a structure that is similar to the structure of a whole text. It has an introduction, a body and a conclusion. The main idea usually can be found in the introduction. It means that if you want to understand quickly what a paragraph is about, it is enough to read only its introduction.

Find the keywords

Keywords are the main words in the question; they contain the most important information. For instance, in a question like "Employers are likely to employ graduates, who…" there are 3 keywords: **employers**, **employ** and **graduates**.
Identify keywords in each question and look for them in the text – the answer will be near. Don't stop after finding just one, continue to scan through the text – there might be more.

Strategy for the Matching headings task

First, read the instructions and the example. If the instructions say that a heading **cannot** be used more than once – cross the heading used in the example out of the list. This way you won't try to use it again by mistake (and believe me, it's a very common mistake!).

Second, return to the map you have prepared. Go over the text and look at your map to see what it says about the idea in the first paragraph. Go to the list of headings and choose the heading that has the meaning that is most similar to the idea on your map, write its number in the margins of the first paragraph. Now continue and do the same for the second paragraph, and so on.

Sometimes you will see that paragraph X *mentions* the same fact as the heading Y, *but only as additional information (not the main idea)*. It is a **trap** to make you choose heading Y for that paragraph X.

It sounds confusing, but this example explains everything:

Paragraph X:
The end result says that 61.6% of the Dutch people vote tegen (against) the European Constitution, while 38.4% voted voor (for) the Constitution. Turnout was unexpectedly high, at 62.8%, more than the last three elections. The 'no' vote follows a similar vote in France last week that led to the resignation of the prime minister Jean-Pierre Raffarin.

Heading Y:
Prime minister of France resigns

Explanation:
Although the resignation of the prime minister of France is mentioned in paragraph X, *it is not its topic*. The topic is the Dutch people voting for/against the constitution, which means that heading Y is not suitable for paragraph X.

If some paragraphs are hard to match – leave them alone, keep moving forward. Come back to them later.

When you have finished matching - check your answers carefully, because they can influence each other. Don't forget to copy the answers to the Answer Sheet.

Strategy for the True/False/Not Given task

To simplify it for you, if the statement **clearly** appears in text - it is True. If the text clearly says the **opposite** of the statement in the question – it is False, if you didn't find the statement to be either TRUE or FALSE – it is Not Given.

Every passage is divided into paragraphs and each paragraph usually contains an **answer to one question**. It means that if you have found an answer to question 1 in paragraph A, then the answer to question 2 will probably be in paragraph B. In many cases, when you don't see that the paragraph is confirming that the statement is either True or False, the answer is Not Given.

The best advice here is not to over think. Otherwise you might start building logical sequences that lead you in the wrong direction.

A trap to watch out for is **explicit answer choices**. The following example demonstrates what I mean:
The text says: "This course is a must for all the first year students, excluding foreign students".
The statement in question is "**All** the first year students have to take this course",
The Answer should be **F**(alse), because there is an exception - foreign students.
All the explicit answers that mean "no exceptions" are a bit suspicious and call for more attention.

Strategy for the Multiple-choice task

Here too the True/False/Not Given technique is a big help. The difference is that you need to use it on each option. For every possible answer you need to decide, if it is True, False or Not Given in the text. Finally, the answers you have marked as False or Not Given are incorrect, and the ones you marked as True are correct.

Remember: it is True only when the passage says exactly the **same** thing, it is False when the passage says exactly the **opposite** and it is Not Given in any other case.

Keep in mind that there are cases when all the choices are correct or none of them is correct. Read the instructions carefully and you will know what to do in such cases.

Strategy for the Gap fills

First of all try to understand what the main idea of the first sentence is. Then find it on your map – this should take you to the paragraph that "hides" the answer.

Now, when you know **where** to look, you need to know **what** to look for. Look at the text around the gap to understand what's missing - a noun (like boy, toy, truck), an adjective (little, pretty, shiny) or a verb (stands, looks, moves).

For example, what is missing here: "She _____ around and saw him in the corner"?

You have 4 choices: happy, man, looked, smiled. It is clear that you need a verb here, but which one, "looked" or "smiled"? Now it is time to start reading the text.
Find where the example answer is and start there. Remember to read only the first, the second and the last sentence. Of course, "looked" is the right word!

Sometimes there are words near a gap that will give you a clue about what kind of word is missing. For example, " The main physical activities in the summer camp are fishing, _____ and swimming. Naturally, you will look for words that end with "ing" to fill the gap – like "hiking".

There are 2 types of gap-fills:

1) There is a **list** of words for you to choose from
2) There is **no list**, you need to choose words from the text

When you choose a word from the list and the instructions say that every word is to be used **once** only, write it above the gap and cross it out from the list. If there is more than one possible answer – write them all and then decide which one is better.

If they don't give you a list, try to pick a word from the text. It is better than "inventing" it, because it saves time and your chances of being right are higher.

After you have decided on the word that goes into the gap, read the whole sentence again. It must make sense according to the text, and it must be grammatically correct.

When you move forward to the second gap, keep in mind that usually there are no more than 2 gaps per paragraph. It means that if you have found the answer to the first gap in paragraph 1, the answer to the second gap will be in paragraph 2 and so on.

Assumptions are the mother of all mess-ups!

Don't assume you know the answer, search for it in the passage. When answering the questions, you must stick to the facts as they are written in the paragraph. Forget all about your personal knowledge and experience! Relying on your own knowledge is the most natural thing for you, so sometimes they use it in IELTS to trick you into making a choice according to what you know or believe and not according to the passage.

Practice, practice, practice!

Reading the text in the way I described in this chapter must become a second nature to you. The only way to make it happen is to practice using my tips while doing the Reading test.

When practicing, finish the Reading test and then check your answers according to the Answer key. Pay attention to those you've got **wrong**, not those you've got right – understand why you didn't do them right and try to remember, so that mistake won't be repeated.

Practice with a clock and copy your answers onto the Answer Sheet. You may use the one from the chapter on the Listening test; it is similar to the Reading test Answer Sheet.

In order to practice, use not only the General Training module tests, but also the Academic module reading tests. This advice has 2 main reasons behind it – there are more Academic texts available to practice on than General Training, and it is a proven strategy to get your score higher, because while hoping for the best you are preparing for the worst. Academic reading is much more difficult than General Training, and if you are ready for Academic – General will be a piece of cake for you.

Normally, you need to buy texts to practice on, but I have managed to find a few sources of free tests and recommend them to you.

http://ielts-blog.com/online-practice/ - choose course type (General/Academic), then click on a big square button that says "FREE"
http://www.ieltsgym.com/?id=FreeEnglishlessons
http://www.ieltshelpnow.com/sample_tutorials.html
http://www.ieltsontrack.com/mini_test.php?module=2

Tips for the Writing test

As you may remember, the Writing test of the General Training Module has 2 tasks:

Writing Task 1 - to write a letter.
Writing Task 2 - to write an essay.

Writing a letter must not take you more than 20 minutes, so there will be 40 minutes left for the essay. Usually, not all of us are good at writing letters, not to mention essays, let alone in English! Well, SURPRISE – there is a technique to it, making writing so simple, a monkey could do it. So let's get down to business.

First, some general guidelines

You will receive two Answer Sheets to write on – one for Writing Task 1, meaning letter, and one for Writing Task 2, meaning essay. Keep your writing neat, clean and nice-looking. Leave a blank line between paragraphs and don't write in the margins of the Answer Sheet. Don't make a mess even if you have made a mistake – just cross it out once.

If there are instructions that say that you need to write about a number of things (let's say A, B, C) – do it, write about every one of them. It is important for your score. You need to show the examiner that you read and understood the instructions; otherwise he or she might think that you didn't. Here is an example of such instructions:

- Describe the situation
- Explain your problem
- Suggest a solution

One of the most typical mistakes is to copy task instructions. It is absolutely forbidden, wastes precious time and people lose points for it. You can use what is written in task instructions only if you write the same in other words.

Task length is very important, so if you cannot reach the required word limit (150 for a letter, 250 for an essay), try to get close to it. A good way to quickly count the number of words in your task is to count the number of words in one line and then multiply by the number of lines.
For example, 10 words in one line x 25 lines = 250 words in total.

These simple rules apply to both letter and essay. Stick to them, and your work will leave a good impression on the examiner.

Tips for Writing Task 1 - Letter

Types of letters

In the test you may be asked to write only one of **4 types** of letters:

- **Complaint / Request (of information) letter**

- **Job application letter**

- **Personal letter**

- **Formal business letter**

There are rules about how to write a letter of each type. When a letter is graded by IELTS examiners, its content, structure, vocabulary and fluency of language are equally important. So I will show you a model for every letter type, followed by phrases and forms of speech, and the only thing you need to do is insert information on your particular topic in it. I will also provide you with examples to demonstrate what your letter should look like.

Complaint

This is a letter you write to complain about something. It could be something you have purchased or bad service that you have received, or an accident that happened to you. You must describe it and demand some appropriate actions from the relevant people.

There are **4 paragraphs** in this type of letter. They should look something like this:

1. Start with "Dear Sir/Madam," (or write the person's name if it was given in task instructions) Explain briefly (in one or two sentences) what you are complaining about.
"I am writing to express my dissatisfaction with a laptop computer that I purchased in your store."

2. Explain in more detail

   a) What happened, what the problem is.
   "I purchased a laptop in your store on 12/3/2015, just 3 days ago. After using it a few times, I noticed the spacebar key was broken".

b) What you are unhappy about.
"I was very surprised to see the newest model with a 2-year warranty breaking so soon and for no reason at all."

c) What you did to resolve the situation.
"I contacted your store immediately in order to return the laptop and spoke to the store manager. He refused to replace the laptop and suggested that it should be repaired."

d) How you feel about the problem.
"You can imagine how receiving this offer upset me."

This paragraph should be the longest in the whole letter. You can even divide it into several parts.

3. Write what you would like them to do, and what you will do if they don't give you what you want.
"I insist that you replace the damaged laptop and send me a new one. Otherwise I will be forced to stop my payments to your store."

4. Write a formal ending for the letter, your name and sign.
"I look forward to hearing from you."
If you **know** the name of the person you are writing to, sign
"Yours **sincerely**,
    Mr. Smith"
If you **don't know** the name of the person you are writing to, sign
"Yours **faithfully**,
    Mr. Smith"

Useful phrases

The following phrases will make your letter look good. In case it is hard for you to remember all of them, choose just one from each paragraph, memorize it and use it for all letters of this type.

<u>For Paragraph 1</u>

- "I am writing to complain about…"
- "I am writing in regard to…"
- "The reason I am writing to you is (a problem with…)"
- "I am writing to express my concern about / dissatisfaction with…"
- "I would like to bring the matter of … to your attention."
- "I would like to draw your attention to …"

<u>For Paragraph 2</u>

- "I was supposed to receive … Unfortunately, that never happened."
- "You can imagine how unhappy I was to discover …"
- "I regret to inform you that your service was below my expectations."
- "When I tried to contact you by phone, no one could give me a sensible answer."
- "I contacted your representative in …. Unfortunately, he denied me the service that I requested."

<u>For Paragraph 3</u>

- "The ideal solution would be … "
- "I hope you can settle this matter by …(doing something)"
- "I insist on getting a refund of …"
- "Please look into this matter as soon as possible."
- "I believe this matter deserves your urgent attention."

Example of a Complaint letter

This example demonstrates what a good letter of complaint should look like. There are notes in the margins, which indicate paragraph numbers as explained on pages 28-29. You don't need to write them in your own letter. It is enough to just leave a blank line between the paragraphs.

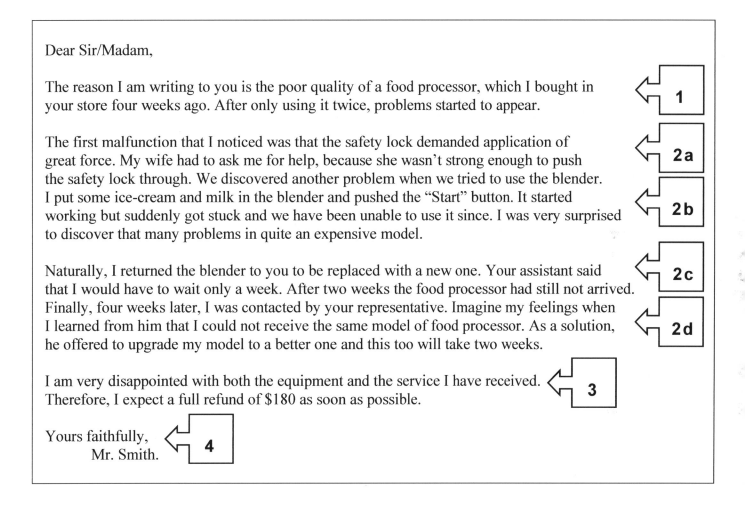

Dear Sir/Madam,

The reason I am writing to you is the poor quality of a food processor, which I bought in your store four weeks ago. After only using it twice, problems started to appear. **1**

The first malfunction that I noticed was that the safety lock demanded application of great force. My wife had to ask me for help, because she wasn't strong enough to push the safety lock through. **2a** We discovered another problem when we tried to use the blender. I put some ice-cream and milk in the blender and pushed the "Start" button. It started working but suddenly got stuck and we have been unable to use it since. I was very surprised to discover that many problems in quite an expensive model. **2b**

Naturally, I returned the blender to you to be replaced with a new one. Your assistant said that I would have to wait only a week. After two weeks the food processor had still not arrived. **2c** Finally, four weeks later, I was contacted by your representative. Imagine my feelings when I learned from him that I could not receive the same model of food processor. As a solution, he offered to upgrade my model to a better one and this too will take two weeks. **2d**

I am very disappointed with both the equipment and the service I have received. Therefore, I expect a full refund of $180 as soon as possible. **3**

Yours faithfully,
    Mr. Smith. **4**

Request of information letter

This is a letter you write to ask a person for information. For example, you may need to receive a train timetable, or a list of books on a certain topic from a library or an itinerary for a trip you have booked to Africa.

There are **3 paragraphs** in this type of letter. They should look something like this:

1. Start with "Dear Sir/Madam," (or write person's name if it was given in task instructions) Explain briefly (in one or two sentences) what kind of information you are interested in. "I am writing to ask for information about a membership in the Shape sports club."

2. Explain in more detail who you are, exactly what information you need, why, when and in what form you need it – a letter, a fax, an e-mail, a phone-call, etc. This should be the longest paragraph of the whole letter.

3. Write a formal ending for the letter, your name and sign it. "I look forward to hearing from you." If you **know the name** of the person you are writing to, sign "Yours **sincerely**,
    Mr. Smith" If you **don't know the name** of the person you are writing to, sign "Yours **faithfully**,
    Mr. Smith"

Example of a Request letter

This example demonstrates what a good letter of request for information should look like. There are notes in the margins, which indicate paragraph numbers as explained on page 32. You don't need to write them in your own letter. It is enough to just leave a blank line between the paragraphs.

Dear Sir/Madam,

I am writing to ask for the itinerary of my trip to Africa that I booked with your company, and for some more details related to my travel.

The trip I am referring to starts on May 12, 2015. I am supposed to leave with a group of 16 people and I would like to find out their names and ages. In addition, I need to know the details of my flights, including the airlines, flight numbers, and departure and arrival times. Details of accommodation are also important to me, in particular the names and locations of the hotels and the basis of bookings (bed and breakfast, half board or full board). I would appreciate it if you sent me a list of optional day trips that are available and their respective prices. Lastly, I require the list of local doctors I can contact in case of an emergency, a phone number for your company representative in Africa, and a receipt for the payment I made to your company on March 28, 2015.

This information can be sent to me by e-mail or fax. I would like to receive it as soon as possible, but no later than a week before my flight.

I look forward to hearing from you.

Yours faithfully,
Mr. Smith

Job application letter

This is a letter you write to apply for a certain position that is vacant. In real life you would attach your resume to it. Of course, you don't have to do it in IELTS, writing the letter is enough.

There are **4 paragraphs** in this type of letter. They should look something like this:

1. Start with "Dear Sir/Madam," (or write a person's name if it was given in task instructions)
   Write what position you are applying for, and where it was advertised.
   "I would like to apply for the position of secretary advertised in 'Herald Tribune' on April 15th, 2015."

2. Write about your skills, diplomas and experience.
   "I am a Software Engineer with more than ten years of experience in …"
   "I graduated in Some Study Course from Famous University, 2001"
   "At present I am employed as a … by a company …"
   "I am familiar with…"
   "My skills include working with …, performing …, managing…"
   "In the course of my present job I have been responsible for planning and the organization of …"
   "I am used to working at a fast pace to meet deadlines".
   As in previous types of letters, this paragraph should be the longest of the whole letter.

3. Explain why you are interested in this job, express your motivation to contribute. Ask to schedule an interview as soon as possible.
   "I would like to apply my skills in your company."
   "I believe the position you are offering will give me the opportunity to..."
   "If you find my skills and experience suitable, please contact me to schedule an interview."
   "I am looking forward to discussing my credentials with you personally."

4. Thank the person.
   "Thank you for your time and consideration."
   If you know the name of the person you are writing to, sign
   "Yours sincerely,
      Mr. Smith"
   If you don't know the name of the person you are writing to, sign
   "Yours faithfully,
      Mr. Smith"

Example of a Job Application letter

Dear Sir/Madam,

I would like to apply for the position of flight attendant, advertised in the October issue of "The Wings" magazine.

As you can see from my CV, I am a flight attendant with 5 years of experience.
I had a one-year apprenticeship with United Airways, and during the following 3 years
I worked for Sky-High Airlines. Last year I was working for AirComfort Airlines,
providing customer service to first class passengers.

I have a pleasant personality and good communication skills. I am familiar with service
and emergency instructions, and am used to working unsupervised. My experience includes
administering first aid to ill passengers and dealing with unusual incidents. I am available
to work on weekends, public holidays or overtime.

If you find my skills and experience suitable, please contact me to schedule an interview. I am
looking forward to discussing my credentials with you personally.

Thank you for your time and consideration.

Yours faithfully,
S. Holts

Personal Letter

A personal letter is usually written to a friend or a relative. It doesn't have many strict rules. I have a couple of suggestions that will make your life easier:

1. Start with something like "Dear Linda," or "My dearest Charlie,"
   Then apologize that you have forgotten to write.
   "I am sorry I haven't written for so long."
   Next, write the purpose of your letter
   "I am writing to thank/tell/ask/apologize/wish…"

2. Start writing on a topic from paragraph 1. Once again, this paragraph must be the longest one. If possible, try to write 2 paragraphs (see 2a and 2b below).

3. Sign : "All the best, Kathy"
   "Yours, Louse"
   "With love and many thanks from me, Diana"

Example of a Personal Letter

Dear Sarah,

I am sorry I haven't written for so long. My work keeps me so busy, that I never have a minute to myself. I am writing to invite you to my wedding. 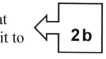 **1**

Since you have never met my future husband, you must have a million questions running through your head right now. I hope I can tell you enough to put your mind at ease until **2a** we meet. Five months ago I decided to take a cruise to the Bahamas, to get away for a little while. And on that cruise it so happened that I met my future husband Alan.
He is the most wonderful, loving person you could ever imagine and we are very happy together.

The wedding will take place at my parents' mansion. The date is October 6th, at 7 o'clock. I am so looking forward to introducing you to Alan, and he can't wait to **2b** meet you, too. I told him all about you and our friendship.

With love, **3**
   Amy.

Formal Business letter

Any letter other than a Complaint, a Request, a Job application, or a Personal letter is a Business letter. It could be an explanation you write to a library about the books that were never returned, or a letter to a Car Rental Company, describing the road accident you were involved in.

There are **4 paragraphs** in this type of a letter. They should look something like this:

1. Start with "Dear Sir/Madam," (or write the person's name if it was given in task instructions) Explain briefly (in one or two sentences) who you are and/or what are you writing about. "I am writing in regard to some books I borrowed from the library on March 15, 2015 and never returned".

2. Explain in more detail the purpose of your letter. Consider the idea that the task instructions give you and write about it. Make up interesting details in addition to the original idea. This should be the longest paragraph of the whole letter.

3. Say what kind of answer you expect or what suggestions you have for the situation. It is also a good place to apologize, if applicable.

4. Write a formal ending for the letter, your name and sign it.
   "I look forward to hearing from you."
   If you **know** the name of the person you are writing to, sign
   "Yours **sincerely**,
       Mr. Smith"
   If you **don't know** the name of the person you are writing to, sign
   "Yours **faithfully**,
       Mr. Smith"

Example of a Formal Business letter

Dear Sir/Madam,

I am writing to apologize for keeping some books that I borrowed from the college library 3 days ago. I am aware that I have had them for too long.

I have found myself in this unpleasant situation for a reason. My close relative was very ill and I had to visit him at hospital. I intended to return the books immediately after I got back to the college, but unfortunately I left the books on a train on my way from the hospital to the library. It will take me two more days to get them back from the "Lost and Found" department at the train station.

I understand that other students may need those books and sincerely apologize for the inconvenience. I will try to return the books as soon as possible. I would appreciate it if you didn't revoke my library privileges, I assure you this will never happen again.

Faithfully yours,
    John Smith.

Do it right!

Now, when you know what a letter should look like, it's time you learned **how to write it fast**. It works for absolutely any kind of letter. After writing a couple of letters you will realize that writing down 150 words alone takes you 15 minutes, plus you have to think of a story to tell in your letter, to make it interesting.

So this is how you do it:

1. When you get the writing assignment, first look and understand what kind of letter you need to write: complaint/request, business, job application or personal.

2. Read the assignment and write down on the draft paper the first three things that come to your mind. Those ideas must refer to the topic directly. If there is a number of things you need to write about, refer to **every one** of them. Make things up, be creative, it doesn't have to be the absolute truth. Stop right there, no more thinking!

3. Start writing. First paragraph requires no thinking – write 1-2 sentences that explain the topic of your letter.

4. Remember the 3 things you made up? Use them while you are writing your second paragraph. Make it the largest paragraph, because this is your only chance to get 150 words in the letter.

5. When paragraph two is done, paragraphs three and four (if applicable) are a piece of cake, because they generally are based on paragraph two.

6. After you have finished writing, read the letter once again and check for grammatical, spelling and punctuation errors.

Practice, practice, practice!

I believe that practicing in writing is a must. Use the following topics to practice writing letters as much as you can. They will also help you understand better how to **classify** the letter tasks – to know what kind of letter you need to write.

To view some sample answers visit the website below:
http://www.ielts-blog.com/ielts-writing-samples-essays-letters-reports/

Complaint letters tasks

Topic 1

You should spend no more than 20 minutes on this task and write at least 150 words.

You have bought a mobile phone in a duty-free shop just a few days ago, and it doesn't work properly.
Write a letter to the manager to complain about it and ask him/her to solve the problem.

You do not need to write your address.
Begin your letter as follows: Dear Sir/Madam,

Topic 2

You should spend no more than 20 minutes on this task and write at least 150 words.

You rented a car from Car Rental Company. The air conditioner has stopped working. You phoned the company a week ago but it still has not been repaired.
Write a letter to the company. In your letter
  * introduce yourself
  * explain the situation
  * say what action you would like the company to take

You do not need to write your address.
Begin your letter as follows: Dear Sir/Madam,

Request of Information letter tasks

Topic 1

You should spend no more than 20 minutes on this task and write at least 150 words.

You are a student who wants to apply to Green Pines College. You are experiencing financial problems at the moment.
Write a letter to the Principal of the College explaining your situation and ask for information on scholarships or other means of financial help available.

You do not need to write your address.
Begin your letter as follows: Dear Sir/Madam,

Topic 2

You should spend no more than 20 minutes on this task and write at least 150 words.

You would like to participate in a work-related seminar in another country.
Write a letter to the person in charge of the seminar and ask for detailed information on the dates, the program, the accommodation and the cost.

You do not need to write your address.
Begin your letter as follows: Dear Sir/Madam,

Job Application letter task

Topic 1

You should spend no more than 20 minutes on this task and write at least 150 words.

You would like to apply for the following job. Write a letter to Mrs. Keller describing your previous experience and explaining why you would be suitable for the job.

Advertisement: Housekeeper required for private home. Experience is necessary. Contact Mrs. D. Keller.

You do not need to write your address.
Begin your letter as follows: Dear Mrs. Keller,

Personal letters tasks

Topic 1

You should spend no more than 20 minutes on this task and write at least 150 words.

You stayed at your friend's house when you participated in a business seminar in Australia. You left a file with important documents in your room.
Write a letter to your friend, describing the file and ask him/her to return it to you by post.

You do not need to write your address.
Begin your letter as follows: Dear ...,

Topic 2

You should spend no more than 20 minutes on this task and write at least 150 words.

You migrated to another country.
Write a letter to your friend to describe your present life and tell him/her why you chose this country.

You do not need to write your address.
Begin your letter as follows: Dear ...,

<u>Business Letter tasks</u>

Topic 1

You should spend no more than 20 minutes on this task and write at least 150 words.

You successfully passed a job interview. You are expected to start on November 15th, but you will not be available on that date.
Write a letter to your new boss, explaining your situation, expressing your concern and suggesting a solution.

You do not need to write your address.
Begin your letter as follows: Dear Sir/Madam,

Topic 2

You should spend no more than 20 minutes on this task and write at least 150 words.

You are a gift shopkeeper.
Write a letter to your supplier, to let him/her know that you won't need the merchandise you have ordered. Explain your situation and suggest a solution.

You do not need to write your address.
Begin your letter as follows: Dear Sir/Madam,

Topic 3

You should spend no more than 20 minutes on this task and write at least 150 words.

You are a secretary, planning a corporate event.
Write a letter to Entertainment Company explaining the kind of party you would like to organize, indicate the date and time of the event and your special requests.

You do not need to write your address.
Begin your letter as follows: Dear Sir/Madam,

Tips for Writing Task 2 - Essay

You don't have to be a writer to write a good essay. This task may look even harder than the letter, but it is only a first impression. Just follow the rules, keep the right structure, use some "smart" words and practice a little. This way you can easily reach a level, where no matter what topic they give you, after 40 minutes you turn out a beautiful 2-page essay and walk out of the room with a huge smile on your face.

Essay structure

Every essay should have this exact structure: **introduction**, **body** and **conclusion**.
It is very important because your grade is affected by it. The introduction usually takes one paragraph, the body – two or three paragraphs and the conclusion – one paragraph.

Essay topics – 3 different kinds

There are only 3 kinds of essay topics in IELTS, let's call them **A, H, S**.

Topic type "**A**" presents an **Argument** and you need to explore pros and cons, reasons for and against, while you support only one side.

Topic type "**H**" presents a **Hidden argument**. These topics usually ask "To what extent …?", "In what way…?", "How has something changed…?"

Topic type "**S**" presents a **Situation** and you need to explore **reasons** why it is what it is, assume what will happen in the future and suggest solutions to problems, if required.

The following **examples** demonstrate the differences between topics of A, H or S kind:

A: "Modern society benefits greatly from computer technology. However, becoming more dependent on computers has its disadvantages. Discuss the threats of computers."
Here the 2 sides of the argument are the advantages and disadvantages of computers.

H: "To what extent should television participate in our children's education?"
What they **really** ask here is whether the television should educate the children or not.

S: "As a result of tourism many unique places in the world are being damaged or even destroyed. Why is this happening? What are some possible solutions to this problem? "
Here you can see the description of a situation and you have to write what you think about it.

Essay of A(rgument) kind

1. **The introduction** paragraph must clearly state the argument, both sides of it. Do not simply copy the topic from the instructions, write it in **other** words. Don't give your opinion, save it for later.

2. **Body** paragraphs (at least 2) must refer to each side of the argument. Write the first paragraph about the side you disagree with. The side you do agree with should be in the **last** body paragraph, because this way it naturally leads to the conclusion.

3. **The conclusion** paragraph should contain a summary of the points you were making. Never mind if the paragraph turns out to be short, the important thing is that you kept the structure of the essay.

Essay of H(idden argument) kind

1. **The introduction** paragraph must define the question. You need to reveal the hidden argument. Rewrite the topic, so it will say what it **really** means:
   from "to what extent something affects…?" **to** "Does something affect…?"
   from "in what way something contributes?" **to** "does something contribute?"
   from "how does something influence…?" **to** "does something influence …?
   Now it is an argument with two sides, and you write essay of kind "**A**".

Essay of S(ituation) kind

1. **The introduction** paragraph must state the situation and explain it. Don't give your opinion here.

2. **Body** paragraphs (at least 2) should describe reasons that have led to the situation being like it is now. Each paragraph should talk about one reason.

3. **The conclusion** paragraph should summarize the key points of the essay. If the task requires suggesting a solution to a problem, recommendations, advice - this is the place for it. If your opinion is required – you should also give it in the conclusion paragraph.

General suggestions

- Write on the given topic directly, don't slide to another theme.

- Write in general, not about your personal experiences, but about what is going on in the world.

- Read the task instructions and write about every little thing that is requested. If the task requires suggesting a solution – do it.
  Don't forget to give recommendations or advice, if requested.

Baby steps through the essay

After you have read all that, you still have no idea how to start writing.
So let's do it together:

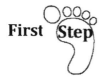 **First Step**

Read and classify the question. You need to decide what kind of topic you have got, an A, H or S. It will affect the way you plan your essay.

Example:

"Home schooling belongs to the past and is unacceptable in modern society. To what extent do you agree or disagree with this statement?
Use your own knowledge and experience and support your arguments with examples and relevant evidence"

We can clearly see a hidden argument here. By revealing the real meaning of the topic we get "Is home schooling acceptable in modern society?" This way it becomes an "A" topic, an argument with 2 sides – for and against home education.

Second 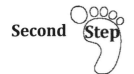 **Step**

Here you need to come up with ideas, thoughts and opinions on the given topic. The best way to do it is to think of some *main* ideas and then to write everything you can think of regarding those ideas. In case you are working on an essay of an "A" or "H" kind, you need to think about ideas for and against the topic. If you are working on an essay of kind "S" – you need to think about the reasons for the situation to be the way it is.

Example:

Let's say that after some thinking you came up with the following ideas, and your opinion is **against** education at home.

For:	Against:
parents know their children	no scientific approach (like associative learning)
learning is more enjoyable	not every parent is capable
children feel safe	parents forgot the material

Now you should think about what goes where in your essay. On the same draft paper where you have written the ideas, group them and decide which paragraph will describe which idea. If the topic is an argument (type A), remember to put the side you don't agree with first and the side you do agree with second. Think about how to move from one paragraph to another. There should be a connective logical sentence that drives you towards the next paragraph's topic.

Example:

Parents know their children	1st body paragraph	side you don't agree with
Learning is more enjoyable	1st body paragraph	
Children feel safe	1st body paragraph	
no scientific approach	2nd body paragraph	side you do agree with
associative learning	2nd body paragraph	
not every parent is capable	3rd body paragraph	side you do agree with
parents forgot the material	3rd body paragraph	

Third Step

It is time to write the answer. According to the plan you have made, start writing the essay. The first sentence of the introduction gives the main idea of the essay, either presenting sides of the argument or describing a situation. The last sentence of the introduction should naturally lead into the first paragraph of the body. Remember to keep the paragraph structure and to connect paragraphs so that one leads to another.

Important! Try to start body paragraphs with a linking word (like However, Therefore, Moreover, Nevertheless, etc.). It raises your score.

Example:

This is an essay written according to the ideas you came up with. The ideas are in bold font for easier understanding.

Everything has two sides and home schooling is not an exception. In the past it seemed like the most natural way of educating children, but today many people criticize it.

*We must acknowledge that **parents know their children best**. That gives them a good chance of knowing how to make their child understand certain concepts. Using their child's interests, parents can make the process of **learning more enjoyable** and effective. In addition, being at home makes a **child feel safe**, which contributes to his ability to concentrate on studying.*

Nevertheless, many people believe that teaching should be done by professionals.
*There are many proven **scientific approaches** that produce good results and without those techniques, parents who teach their kids at home have no chance of success. **Associative learning** is a good example of such a technique. Showing the child images while learning the alphabet (apple for "a", boy for "b") makes him or her remember the letters faster and easier.*

*In addition, **not every parent is capable** of teaching his or her child at home because the blind cannot lead the blind. Parents cannot teach children something they don't know themselves, and let's face it - not all of us have a profound knowledge of history or geography even on a school textbook level. Eventually, even those mums and dads who succeeded at school could **forget material** with the passage of time.*

In conclusion, I have more trust in the abilities and experience of professional teachers than I do in my own.

And finally - **read the essay carefully from the beginning and check it for errors.**

40 minutes? Not enough!

Hardly anyone can get their first essays done on time. So don't be disappointed if it takes you an hour or even longer. First try to get used to the Baby Steps process that I explained earlier. After a little bit of practice, you will start writing essays faster and faster, and finally you will reach your goal - an essay in 40 minutes. You should work with a clock all the time - this is the only way for you to monitor your progress.

Helpful phrases

Usually people who don't read and write in English every day have trouble expressing themselves in an essay. So I enclose here a list of phrases to help you write more elegant sentences.

Phrases to show two sides of an argument

- "Some people prefer …. Those who disagree point out that…"
- "We must acknowledge … Nevertheless, …"
- "No one can deny … However, …"
- "Many people hold the opinion… Others, however, disagree…"
- "Although it is hard to compete with …, some people still prefer …"

Phrases for adding a linked point

- "Not only…, but…"
- "Also"
- "Furthermore,"
- "In addition,"
- "Moreover,"

Phrases to contrast with what was written before

- "Although…"
- "However,"
- "Nevertheless,"
- "Even if…"
- "In spite of"
- "On the other hand"

Phrases for examples

- "For example,"
- "For instance,"
- "In particular,"
- "…, such as"
- "To illustrate …"

Phrases for results

- "As a result"
- "Therefore"
- "Thus"
- "So"
- "Eventually"

Phrases for conclusion

- "Lastly,"
- "Finally,"
- "To conclude with,"
- "In short,"
- "In conclusion,"

Practice, practice, practice!

My advice would be to practice on essays as much as you can. Your goal is to be able to write an essay of 250 words in 40 minutes on any given topic. The topic doesn't matter, the important thing is that you know and implement the techniques you've learned.

So for those of you who don't take chances, the following list of topics is similar to those you will get in IELTS. Practice with a clock and count the number of words.

To view some sample answers visit the website below:
http://www.ielts-blog.com/ielts-writing-samples-essays-letters-reports/

Enjoy!

Topic 1   *(Hint: Argument)*

You are advised to spend the maximum time (40 minutes) on this task.

Even though globalization affects the world's economies in a very positive way, its negative side should not be forgotten. Discuss.

You should write at least 250 words.

Topic 2   *(Hint: Hidden Argument)*

You are advised to spend the maximum time (40 minutes) on this task.

Some people say that the education system is the only critical factor in the development of a country. To what extent do you agree or disagree with this statement?

You should write at least 250 words.

Topic 3   *(Hint: Argument)*

You are advised to spend the maximum time (40 minutes) on this task.

Dieting can change a person's life for the better or ruin one's health completely. What is your opinion?

You should write at least 250 words.

Topic 4 *(Hint: Hidden Argument)*

You are advised to spend the maximum time (40 minutes) on this task.

Education in financial management should be a mandatory component of the school program. To what extent do you agree or disagree with this statement?

You should write at least 250 words.

Topic 5 *(Hint: Argument)*

You are advised to spend the maximum time (40 minutes) on this task.

The best way to reduce the number of traffic accidents is to raise the age limit for younger drivers and to lower the age limit for elderly ones. Do you agree?

You should write at least 250 words.

Topic 6 *(Hint: Situation)*

You are advised to spend the maximum time (40 minutes) on this task.

Obesity was once considered a disease of adults; however, it is becoming increasingly common among children. Why do you think this is happening? What can be done to help children stay healthy?

You should write at least 250 words.

Tips for the Speaking test

Finally, we have reached the fun part of IELTS. Many people agree that the secret of success in the Speaking test is being a confident and creative person. Does it mean that others will fail? Not at all! This test is **PREDICTABLE**. Use the following tips to prepare yourself for what's coming and the confidence will come.

What are they looking for?

If you know what is important to IELTS examiners, it improves your chances of success. These guidelines refer to every part of the Speaking test. Stick to them and you will satisfy your examiner.

- Speak without long pauses (when you are trying to think of something to say)

- Understand what the examiner asks you and confirm that by answering accordingly.

- Demonstrate how many "smart" words you know.

- Use all the tenses when you speak - past, present, future – and use them correctly.

- Pronounce the words correctly. For example the word "culture" should sound like "kolcher", not "kultur".

- Important! Accent has nothing to do with pronunciation, so it will not affect your score.

Keep it simple!

This tip refers to the whole Speaking test. Don't start long and complicated sentences if you don't know how to finish them! Keep your sentences simple, and words - understandable. If you make a grammatical error – it's ok to correct yourself, but don't overdo it, you must sound fluent.

When you hear a question, your mind automatically develops an image with the answer. You can describe this image in your own language, but when you start to describe it in English, suddenly you don't have enough words in your vocabulary. So try to think of what part of that image you **can** describe, do it and stop there. Don't let yourself show what words you don't know by saying incomplete sentences.

Interview

The first part of the Speaking test is the Interview. You enter the room, see the examiner, say "Good afternoon!" and smile. He or she asks to see your passport and invites you to sit down. If he/she offers to shake your hand - do it, otherwise - don't.
Your body language is important here, it must show that you are relaxed and confident. When you are talking, try to make eye contact with the examiner as much as you can.

During the interview the examiner asks you questions about yourself, your work, studies, parents, brothers/sisters, pets, etc. Your answer to each question should consist of one or two sentences; try not to answer with just "yes" or "no". After all it's your English they want to hear.

This is an easy task to prepare for. Read the following questions and answers carefully, and you will get a very clear picture of what will happen.

Possible questions and answers

1. **Where do you come from?**
   I live in Smallville. It is a big city /small town located in the south of NeverNeverLand.

2. **What is your home like?**
   I rent an apartment. We have two bedrooms, one living room, one kitchen and of course one restroom. The apartment is not very big, about 70 square meters.

3. **What do you like or dislike about your home?**
   The advantage is that my accommodation has lots of sunlight from the windows. And the disadvantage is that it is noisy because the centre of the city is nearby.

4. **Tell me about your family.**
   I have a mother, a father and a brother. My mother is a social worker, my father is a civil engineer and my brother is a student.

5. **Tell me about your job.**
   Well, I work for a big firm /small company named BananaSoft. It is located in Smallville. My job title is Software Designer.

6. **Is there anything you dislike about your job?**
   Normally, I enjoy my job very much. But sometimes my boss gives me boring assignments, which I don't like at all.

7. What are your plans for the future?
I would like to improve my English first and then find another job with a better salary.

8. What type of transport do you use most?
There are 2 types of transport that I use: I either drive my car or take the bus.

9. Do you like reading?
Yes I do. I enjoy reading very much. Usually, I read every other day of the week.

10. What do you most like to read?
I enjoy reading newspapers, magazines and of course my favorite fantasy books.

11. What kind of television programs do you watch?
Well, my favorite channel is Some TV Channel. I find it very interesting and educational.

12. Tell me about a film you have seen recently
I saw "Some New Movie" a week ago. It is a comedy and I like comedies. This one has some silly jokes but other than that I enjoyed it.

13. Do you have a pet?
Yes I do. I have a dog named Richy. He is 4 years old.

14. What kind of food do you like?
I prefer Asian cooking, mostly Chinese. My favorite dish is noodles with vegetables.

15. How often do you go shopping?
Well, I don't like shopping, so I do it only when I have to.

16. What is your favorite festival and why?
I like October Fest. It's a German festival that starts in late September and ends in October. People drink lots of beer at October Fest and that is why I like it.

17. How do people celebrate this festival?
Well, they build pavilions and stands that sell beer and all kinds of food, a lot of bands are playing there. People from all around Europe come to celebrate the October Fest dressed in traditional German clothes.

Speech

After you have finished the Interview, the examiner will hand you a card with 3 or 4 questions on it. Usually the card asks you to describe a place, an event or a situation from your experience. You have 1 minute to prepare a short speech that answers all of the questions on a card. You also receive a sheet of paper and a pen to write your notes.

The speech should take from one to two minutes. In the end, the examiner might ask you a couple of additional questions.

The tricky part here is to know when 2 minutes have passed. You need to get a feeling what is it like to talk for 2 minutes. My suggestion is to practice at home with a clock, recording yourself while you are speaking on a particular topic. You can use MP3 players that can record. This way you can evaluate your own speech without any help from other people.

Example

Let's take the following topic card and see what kind of speech you could give:

> Describe a journey you went on. You should include in your answer:
>
> - Where you went on your journey
>
> - Why you went to this particular place
>
> - What did you do and with whom
>
> - Whether you enjoyed your journey or not and why

Possible answer:

> "I would like to tell you about a journey I went on a year ago. My wife and I took a trip to Holland.
>
> Both of us wanted to visit Amsterdam very much because we had seen pictures and heard stories from friends about how beautiful and wonderful it is. So finally we bought plane tickets, booked a hotel, packed our bags and our trip began.
>
> We spent a lot of time before our holiday researching all the interesting places to visit and all the sights to see. So we went to the Amstell Beer museum, took a romantic sunset cruise along the canals, drove to Volendam, a really pretty, small fishing village, and visited a cheese farm. Every evening we took long walks along the canals, stopping to rest in small gardens, which Amsterdam has a lot of. Street artists were performing everywhere and a lot of people came to watch.
>
> We enjoyed everything we did very much and especially being together in such a beautiful country. Having my wife by my side on this trip made it even more fun."

Practice, practice, practice

I have included here a selection of cards for you to practice on. Choose a card, prepare for 1 minute, writing down the points you will speak about. When you start speaking, try not to get in trouble – don't use words unless you know what they mean, don't use long complicated sentences where you get lost in words. Try to speak simply and make it sound interesting.

Describe a book that has had a major influence on you.
You should include in your answer:

- What the book's title is and who wrote it
- How you first heard of it
- What the book is about
- Why it has played such an important role in your life

Describe your favorite restaurant. You should include in your answer:

- Where it is located in the city
- What it looks like inside and outside
- What kind of food is served there
- What makes this restaurant so special to you and others

Describe a museum you visited. You should mention in your answer:

- Where this museum is situated
- Why people visit the museum
- What it looked like
- Why you liked this museum

Describe a conflict at work you once had. You should mention:

- The nature of the conflict
- Why the conflict occurred
- What you felt at the time of the conflict
- What you had to do to resolve it

Discussion

In the third sub-part of the test you have a discussion with the examiner. The topic is somehow related to the one from section two, but it is about ideas that are more abstract. Your job is to express and justify an opinion. It is called a discussion, but in reality *you are the one who does most of the talking*.

To give you an idea of what it will be like, here is a card you might get in part 2 of the Speaking test:

Describe a good friend of yours. You should say

- Where and when you met
- What you do together
- What you like about him/her, and
- Why she/he is a good friend of yours

Then in the third sub-part of the Speaking test the examiner may ask you this kind of questions:

- What sort of person would you not be able to have as a good friend?
- What do you value and not value in people?
- Can people, opposite in personality, be good friends?
- What do children think about friendship? What about adults? Compare them.
- What do you think of friendship formed through the internet? What good and bad aspects does it have?

Have an opinion!

Now that you have got the idea, how do you prepare for this kind of test?
Well, you need to have an opinion on a wide range of different topics.

I include here a list of some of the most common topics for you to think about.
Just go over them, think of what you have to say on those issues and think of which words you will use. Then record yourself saying a couple of sentences on each of the topics and listen to what comes out. Think of what you could have done better. This should get you ready for the Discussion part.

You can view the latest topics from real IELTS exams in the website below:
http://www.ielts-blog.com/category/recent-ielts-exams/

And this is a summary of topics for you to think about:

General topics

o   The main industry in your country now, how it will develop in the future.
o   Effects of pollution on ecology.
o   Popular forms of transport in your country.
o   How to improve public transport.
o   How your country has been improved.
o   The city you are living in, its advantages and disadvantages.
o   Your country's weather, main seasons.
o   Your country's animals, in what ways they are used.
o   A piece of equipment that you consider very important, why, how you started to use it.
o   Computers - their advantages and disadvantages, whether people of different sexes and ages use them more or less.
o   Food in restaurants, why and when we eat there, what are the pros and cons of eating in a restaurant.
o   Celebrities in your country.
o   Idols - who chooses them, who copies them, etc.
o   A favorite holiday in your country

Household

o   Who does the shopping?
o   Where do you like to shop and when?
o   What do you shop for?
o   Who does the housework, which work is the most important, why?

About yourself

o   How do you like spending your time?

o   Favorite movies(films), do you watch them on TV or in the .cinema?

o   Would you like to act in movies? Why not?

o   Where you like to spend your vacation

o   Study or work, where, what do you like most about your job, what do you dislike about your job?

o   Your future plans

o   Your hobbies

o   Do you think free time is important and why?

o   What did you study at university?

o   Which subject is your favorite?

o   Which subject don't you like?

o   What do you want to do in the future?

o   Your favorite food

o   The greatest success in your life

o   Design of your apartment, likes, dislikes, why?

o   The room you like most, what you do there most, what it looks like?

o   Your favorite sportsmen.

o   Favorite TV program.

o   Most interesting time in your life.

Things that were important in your life

o   An important song

o   An important book - what was it about, how did it influence you?

o   A doll or some other toy, who gave it to you, on what occasion, what did you do with it?

Friends

- o   Who is your best friend?
- o   Where and when did you meet?
- o   What do you like the best about him/her?
- o   What have you done together? Explain the reasons why you have a strong friendship.
- o   What do children think about friendship? What about adults? Compare them.
- o   What sort of person would you not be able to have as a good friend?
- o   Can people, opposite in personality, be good friends?
- o   What do you value and not value in people?
- o   Friendship through the Internet, good and bad sides.

Traveling

- o   How can a visitor travel in my country?
- o   How did your grandparents travel in the past?
- o   Will the travel method change in the future?
- o   Traveling in a group compared with traveling on your own.
- o   What kinds of holidays exist?
- o   Where people prefer to go on vacation.
- o   Developments that have a positive effect on the growth of tourism.

Toys

- o   Why boys and girls chose different toys
- o   Why toys are good for kids
- o   Negative influence of toys, educational side of toys

Music

- o   What kind of music do you like?
- o   Why we should teach music to our kids.

What if …?

It can happen that the examiner asks you a question and you don't have a clue what he/she is talking about. Don't panic! Just say:

- I am not sure what you mean, could you be more specific?
- Could you repeat the question, please?

If you don't have a ready answer and you are trying to borrow some time, say:

- Well, I've never thought about that, but I would say that…
- Well, it is not a simple question.

If they ask for your opinion, you can start by saying:

- In my opinion…
- I think that…
- Well, if you ask me, …
- When it comes to me, I …

You will probably have to speak in present, past and future tenses. When asked to speak about the future, say:

- I am sure that (something will/won't happen)
- It is likely/unlikely that (some event will / won't occur)

Leave a good impression

FINALLY!!! When leaving the room after the interview, look the examiner in the eyes, smile and simply say: *"Thank you for your time. Good bye"*.

Isn't life great? :)

Pocket tips

Listening
- Read instructions.
- Guess what is missing: is it a word, a place, a name, a number, how many?
- Divide questions into groups.
- Listen for details.
- Anything said loud and clear could be an answer, whispered - not an answer.
- Repetition and dictation – answer.
- Multiple choices – use T/F/NG method to eliminate all choices but one.
- Gap fills – look around the gaps for clues (Bad grammar = wrong answer).
- Traps: Change of mind, generalization.
- Copy answers: just the letter, not the circle,
  just your answer, not the whole sentence.

Reading
- Read instructions
- Manage your time.
- Make a map.
- Easy questions first – complicated second.
- Look for keywords.
- Matching headings – use the map.
- T/F/NG: Clearly said = True
          Opposite to what is said = False
          Not what is said = Not Given
- Multiple Choices – use T/F/NG method to eliminate all choices but one.
- Gap fills – use the map to find where the answer is hiding.
- Don't make assumptions!
- Have time left – check your answers.

Speaking

Interview:	Be confident and relaxed
	Eye contact with the examiner
	Answer every question with at least 2 sentences
Speech:	Write down main points
	Speak simply - no big words if you aren't sure how to use them
	Make it sound interesting
Discussion:	Have an opinion on everything
	Any opinion is acceptable (no "good" or "bad" opinions)
	In the end, thank the examiner and shake hands

Writing

Letters:

Complaint	Request of information

Complaint

1. What are you complaining about?
2. a) What is the problem?
   b) Why is that a problem?
   c) What did you do to resolve the situation?
   d) What was the result?
3. What do you want to be done?
4. Faithfully Yours,
   Smith

Request of information

1. What info do you need in general?
2. a) Who are you?
   b) What exactly do you need to know?
3. How do you want to get this info: a phone call, an e-mail, a fax, a letter?
4. Faithfully Yours,
   Smith

Business

1. What is the general purpose of this letter?
2. a) Who you are (introduce yourself)
   b) Why do you write this letter (details)?
3. What kind of answer do you expect? Suggestions, solutions, etc.
4. Faithfully Yours,
   Smith

Job application

1. What position are you applying for?
2. What are your skills, diplomas, experience?
3. a) Why do you want this job?
   b) You want to get an interview
4. Thanks for consideration,
   Faithfully Yours,
   Smith

Essay:

3 types of topics: Argument, Hidden argument, Situation

Plan for Argument and Hidden Argument topic type (5 paragraphs)

1. Introduction – 2 sides of the argument
2. Write about the side you don't agree with
3. Write about the side you do agree with
4. Write more about the side you agree with
5. Conclusion – sum up, suggestions, solutions.

Plan for Situation topic type (5 paragraphs)

1. Introduction par.– define the situation
2. Write about reason # 1 for the situation
3. Write about reason # 2 for the situation
4. Write about reason # 3 for the situation
5. Conclusion – sum up, suggestions, solutions.

Study Plan

All the tips I have shared with you so far are priceless, but they will be worth even more if you use them while practicing. As I said before, there are those who study and don't pass, and there are those who don't study and pass. And then there are people like us – we study a little, and then ACE the IELTS!

My advice is: if you have decided to take the IELTS test, give yourself a month of studying according to this plan and go ACE the IELTS right away! Don't wait, don't take long breaks between studying, give it your all – and the success will follow.

There follows a suggested study plan for 21 days that should help you get the best IELTS score you can with your current level of English. All of the IELTS tasks appear in equal proportion. You can change that by doing more of the tasks you feel weak at and removing some (not all!) of the tasks you feel strong at. Remember, it is important to practice in all the tasks and not concentrate just on the ones you fear most.

In this book I have included Writing 1 (letter) and Writing 2 (essay) tasks, interview questions, topic cards and themes for the Speaking test. At the end of the book there is also a full IELTS-like practice test. Additional material for studying (audio files for the Listening test, texts for the Reading test, etc) can be found on the following very helpful internet sites:

For the Listening test

http://ielts-blog.com/online-practice/ - choose course type (General/Academic), then click on a big square button that says "FREE"
http://www.ieltsgym.com/?id=FreeEnglishlessons - online exercises with answers
http://www.esl-lab.com/- for this one you will need a Real Audio Player
http://www.ieltsontrack.com/mini_test.php?module=1 - a test with a transcript

For the Reading test

http://ielts-blog.com/online-practice/ - choose course type (General/Academic), then click on a big square button that says "FREE"
http://www.ieltsgym.com/?id=FreeEnglishlessons
http://www.ieltshelpnow.com/sample_tutorials.html
http://www.ieltsontrack.com/mini_test.php?module=2

For the Writing and Speaking tests

http://www.ielts-blog.com/ielts-writing-samples-essays-letters-reports/
http://www.ielts-blog.com/category/recent-ielts-exams/
http://www.ieltshelpnow.com/ielts-speaking-samples

And of course there are many others, just look up the words "IELTS" and "forum" in any search engine. The internet moves so quickly, by the time you are reading this book there might be many new forums I have never heard of. If you find them or my links are not good any more – please let me know, I will update them and you will receive a FREE up-to-date copy of this book.

Day	Tasks	Time	Remarks
1	Speaking Listening Writing 2 (type A)	30 minutes 30 minutes 60 minutes	Take a 5-10 minute break between tasks
2	Writing 1 (Complaint) Listening Reading	30 minutes 30 minutes 60 minutes	Take a 5-10 minute break between tasks
3	Speaking Listening Writing 2 (type S)	30 minutes 30 minutes 60 minutes	Take a 5-10 minute break between tasks
4	Writing 1 (Request) Listening Reading	30 minutes 30 minutes 60 minutes	Take a 5-10 minute break between tasks
5	Speaking Writing 2 (type A)	30 minutes 60 minutes	Take a 5-10 minute break between tasks
6	Writing 1 (Business) Listening Reading	30 minutes 30 minutes 60 minutes	Take a 5-10 minute break between tasks
7	Speaking Writing 2 (type S)	30 minutes 60 minutes	Take a 5-10 minute break between tasks
8	Writing 1 (Job application) Listening Reading	30 minutes 30 minutes 60 minutes	Take a 5-10 minute break between tasks
9	Speaking Listening Writing 2 (type A)	30 minutes 30 minutes 60 minutes	Take a 5-10 minute break between tasks
10	Writing 1 (Personal) Reading Listening	30 minutes 60 minutes 30 minutes	Take a 5-10 minute break between tasks
11	Speaking Writing 2 (type S) Reading	30 minutes 40 minutes 60 minutes	Take a 5-10 minute break between tasks
12	Writing 1 (Complaint) Reading Listening	30 minutes 60 minutes 30 minutes	Take a 5-10 minute break between tasks

Day	Tasks	Time	Remarks
13	Speaking Listening Writing 2 (type A)	30 minutes 30 minutes 40 minutes	Take a 5-10 minute break between tasks
14	Writing 1 (Business) Reading	30 minutes 60 minutes	Take a 5-10 minute break between tasks
15	Full IELTS test: Listening Reading Writing 1 Writing 2 Speaking	40 minutes 60 minutes 20 minutes 40 minutes 15 minutes	Don't take any breaks, continue through the whole test
16	Listening Writing 2	30 minutes 40 minutes	Take a 5-10 minute break between tasks
17	Speaking Writing 2 (type S)	30 minutes 40 minutes	Take a 5-10 minute break between tasks
18	Writing 1 (Personal) Reading Speaking	20 minutes 60 minutes 30 minutes	Take a 5-10 minute break between tasks
19	Speaking Writing 1 (Business) Listening	30 minutes 20 minutes 30 minutes	Take a 5-10 minute break between tasks
20	Writing 2 (type A) Reading	40 minutes 60 minutes	Take a 5-10 minute break between tasks
21	Full IELTS test: Listening Reading Writing 1 Writing 2 Speaking	40 minutes 60 minutes 20 minutes 40 minutes 15 minutes	Don't take any breaks, continue through the whole test

FULL IELTS PRACTICE TEST

GENERAL TRAINING LISTENING PRACTICE TEST

Visit the following webpage to download the Listening Test recording:
http://www.ielts-blog.com/book-practice-test/

SECTION 1   Questions 1 – 10

Questions 1 – 5

Complete Apollo Car Rentals' new rental form below.
Write NO MORE THAN THREE WORDS AND/OR A NUMBER from the listening for each answer.

Apollo Car Rentals New Rental Form	
Example: Length of Rental	**5 days**
Client's Name	**(1)** _____ Anderson
Age	**(2)** _____
Address	28 Woodland Close, Hightown
Postcode	**(3)** _____
Mobile Telephone	07734 618 223
Payment Method	**(4)** _____
Rental Dates	21st - 25th May
Car Size	**(5)** _____
Price	£240

Questions 6 – 10

Answer the questions below. Use NO MORE THAN THREE WORDS AND/OR A NUMBER from the listening for each answer.

6   What will Carol find in the glove compartment to help her in case of an accident?
7   What's the fuel tank capacity of Carol's rental car?
8   Where is Carol going to leave her car when she's finished with it?
9   What does Ben give Carol for free?
10   How far is *The Haven* hotel from the airport?

SECTION 2   Questions 11 – 20

Questions 11 – 14

Complete the sentences below.

Use NO MORE THAN THREE WORDS from the listening for each answer.

11   The Youth Club's opening hours are from _____ p.m. to 11 p.m.
12   The _____ of six individuals is responsible for the administration of the Youth Club.
13   New _____ are always needed to help improve services, even for a short time.
14   A combination of membership, admittance fees, and help from the _____, individuals and local companies, make up the funding for the Youth Club.

Questions 15 – 20

Complete the table below.

Write NO MORE THAN TWO WORDS AND/OR A NUMBER from the listening for each answer.

Activity	When	Notes
The Homework Club	Weekday evenings From 4.00 p.m.	* 2 hours long * Quiet environment * 2 members of **(15)** _____ are always there
Basketball	Tuesdays and Thursdays 6 p.m. - 7.30 p.m.	* Takes place in the club's 2 sports halls * 2 coaches - 1 from the local pro team, the other from the local secondary school * Frequent **(16)** _____ are organized
Music Evenings	Tuesdays, Thursdays and Fridays 7 p.m. - 9 p.m.	* Come early as very popular * Free music studio * 3 local DJ's help out + local **(17)** _____ teach the children
Dramatic Arts	Mondays and Wednesdays 6.30 p.m. - 10 p.m.	* Volunteers teach drama and **(18)** _____ to the children * Regular performances held
Visits from the **(19)** _____	Periodic	* Talks and advice on alcohol, drugs, crime and other things * Children can ask questions
Overnight Hiking Trips	From time to time	* Skilled adults supervise * Children learn outdoor skills - camping, cooking food, use of **(20)** _____ and a compass * Children gain important character strengths

SECTION 3   Questions 21 – 30

Questions 21 – 26

Complete the student notes below on the second year linguistics course.

Write NO MORE THAN TWO WORDS from the listening for each answer.

The Second Year Linguistic Course

Delivered as lectures, supervision, essays and **(21)** _____ - attendance at all is compulsory.

The number of topics studied depends on which chosen.

Topics

Phonetics	* Study of practical, acoustic and clinical phonetics, speech perception and phonological theories. * Focus on connecting theory to practical speech, and data analysis, special focus on **(22)** _____. * Compulsory.

Clinical Linguistics	* Prepares students for work with communication problems in:
	     - **(23)** _____ with language or hearing problems.
	     - people who've had a stroke.

Onomastics	* The study of origins and development of English **(24)** _____. * Their special properties. * An enjoyable course. * Not the best for jobs, but there are possibilities in **(25)** _____ and advertising.
Sociolinguistics	* Taught by Professor Cotton. * The study of the relationship between people and society. * How the relationship causes **(26)** _____. * How age, geography, media and the language system influence speech.

Questions 27 - 30

Complete the flow chart that summarises the process of writing a dissertation.

Use NO MORE THAN ONE WORD from the listening for each answer.

The Dissertation Process

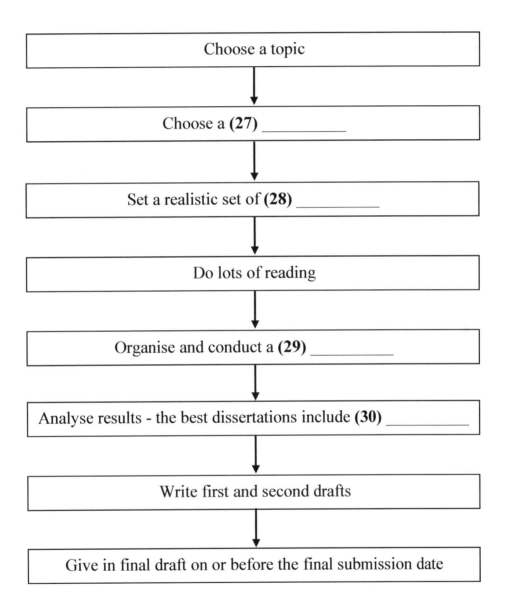

Choose a topic

↓

Choose a **(27)** _____

↓

Set a realistic set of **(28)** _____

↓

Do lots of reading

↓

Organise and conduct a **(29)** _____

↓

Analyse results - the best dissertations include **(30)** _____

↓

Write first and second drafts

↓

Give in final draft on or before the final submission date

SECTION 4 Questions 31 – 40

Questions 31 – 38

Complete the notes below. Use NO MORE THAN TWO WORDS from the listening for each answer.

Endangered Sharks in Australia

Out of 400 species of shark worldwide, 180 are in Australia in all coastal habitats, including even a few sharks in some **(31)** _____ habitats.

The two most endangered sharks in Australia are the grey nurse shark and speartooth shark - both are on the **(32)** _____ .

The Grey Nurse Shark	* 2 separate populations. * Not the man-eater its reputation gives - not usually dangerous unless provoked. * Often blamed for attacks because of its **(33)** _____ , which has led to lots of killing of the shark.
The Speartooth Shark	* Little research done due to lack of specimens, its rarity and confusion in the **(34)** _____ of it and other species. * Similar to northern river shark and the bull shark; the latter often shares the same environment for its **(35)** _____ . * Speartooth very vulnerable to exploitation. * Threats include fishing (commercial and recreational), netting and deterioration of its **(36)** _____ .

Beach Nets

Beach protecting shark nets lead to many shark deaths and are found in many countries affected by shark attacks. Beach nets target sharks potentially dangerous to humans and reduce the shark populations to reduce the attacks. The nets' large **(37)** _____ specifically target sharks. Nets also involve "bycatch", which can include killing other **(38)** _____ , like sea turtles, dugongs, dolphins and whales. One way to avoid bycatch is to use drumlines.

Questions 39 and 40

Complete the diagram below of a drumline set-up.

Write NO MORE THAN THREE WORDS from the listening for each answer.

Drumline Set-up

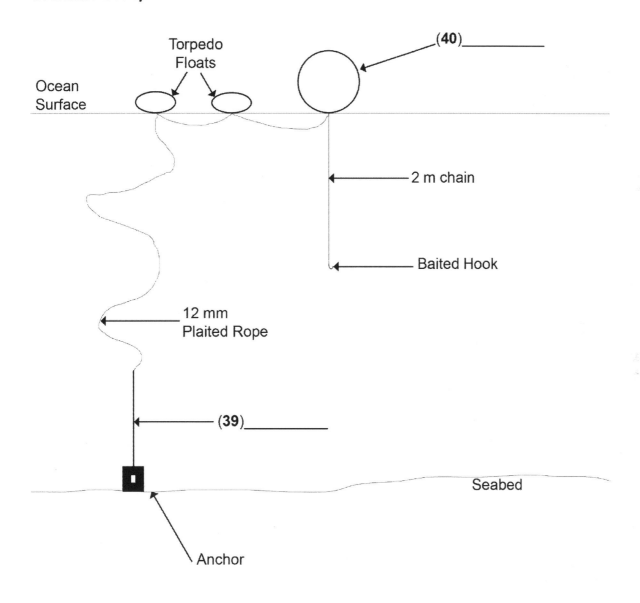

GENERAL TRAINING READING PRACTICE TEST

SECTION 1   Questions 1 – 14

Questions 1 – 9

There are 5 short travel book reviews, A – E, on the next page.

Which review mentions the following information?

Write the correct letter, A - E, in boxes 1 - 9 on your answer sheet.

1   This is written by an organisation and not an individual.

2   This gives advice on cheap places to stay.

3   This focuses on holidays that do not damage the environment.

4   This will tell readers how to deal with the bureaucratic necessities of working in New Zealand.

5   It is advised that the reader does not need to read the whole book.

6   This will tell you how long it will take you to travel between two major New Zealand cities.

7   This is aimed at younger travellers of New Zealand.

8   This gives some information on New Zealand's animal and plant life.

9   This mentions that the New Zealand weather is not always very good.

Travel Books on New Zealand

A   *Hitchhiking Around New Zealand* - Peter Mitchell

Hitchhiking is a great way to see New Zealand up close and personal, but make sure you have some time on your hands, as Mitchell points out that hitchhiking is not often a way of travelling that sticks to timetables. Mitchell also points out that the New Zealand weather can sometimes be poor and he gives good advice on what and how to pack on a holiday of this type. This book is not strong on the major cities, but is excellent as a guide for the smaller towns and villages and things to do with sections on budget places to stay away from the noise of the metropolises. Hitchhiking is often seen as a less expensive way of travelling and this book's price reflects that too, as it's the best deal of those we are reviewing today.

B   *Fishing Holidays in New Zealand* - Tim Jarvis

New Zealand is a wonderfully unspoiled country to go fishing in. In this detailed book, Tim Jarvis covers many of the famous and not so famous places to fish in New Zealand. Unusually for many fishing books, Jarvis covers both sea and river fishing, which makes the book quite a long read, though of course, readers only need to look at the areas that interest them. A particular advantage of this guide is that not only does it tell readers about the best places to fish, it also goes into where to obtain licences and how much they cost.

C   *New Zealand Travel and Touring Map* - Driving Club of New Zealand

Not an actual guide book, but a great travel resource. This detailed driving map will help you plan your New Zealand driving holiday. The map has distance and travel times between the major towns, the locations of petrol stations, the locations of motels, the locations of camp sites, as well as other useful places. The map is double-sided with the North Island on one side and the South Island on the other. The map's dimensions are: 500 mm by 680 mm.

D   *Gap Year New Zealand* - Anna Maw

This book is for any young people thinking of visiting, working, studying or generally living in New Zealand for one or two years. Readers can find out how to find a job, how to obtain a work permit, how to open a bank account, how to get a social security number and lots of other things that are vital for young people spending their gap year in New Zealand.

E   *Adventure Time New Zealand* - Natalie McLoughlin

This guide focuses on adventure and eco-travel - a way of travelling that doesn't hurt the natural habitat or the local people - and includes activities like boating, caving, rafting, kayaking, whale watching, biking, hiking, rock climbing, and wildlife excursions. It also gives background on the area's history (both natural and cultural), the native fauna and flora, and basic travel information, such as hotels, restaurants, and shopping. This book makes it easy to tailor individual excursions with options for every taste.

Questions 10 - 14

Read the text on the following page and choose the correct letter A, B, C or D.

Write the correct letter in boxes 10 - 14 on your answer sheet.

10   Children taking swimming lessons must

A   have basic swimming skills before they start.
B   be members of Brockdale Sports Centre.
C   be watched by their parents.
D   be a minimum of 5 years' old.

11   Parents putting their children onto the swimming classes' waiting list

A   have to pay a small returnable deposit.
B   must do so before the end of November.
C   are usually unsuccessful in getting their children the lessons.
D   must do so during term time.

12   Junior gym sessions are

A   available during term time and holidays.
B   unsupervised, so a parent should be present.
C   sometimes available at weekends.
D   followed by an assessment to check children's progress.

13   Football training is

A   only run during term time.
B   held on the centre's outdoor football pitches.
C   divided into age group sessions.
D   always over-subscribed.

14   Children's parties are

A   only possible at weekends.
B   catered for by a trusted local restaurant.
C   limited to 30 guests.
D   not only for children who are members of Brockdale Sports Centre.

Brockdale Sports Centre - Activities for Children

Swimming

We run swimming lessons throughout the year for children of different ages and swimming ability. Children have to be members to enrol in the swimming classes. We also run classes for parents and their toddlers - lessons usually start from 3 years of age. Lessons for adults can also be arranged. Swimming lessons for children are organised in line with school term times. The closing date for the spring lessons is the last day of November, the closing date for the summer lessons is the last day in March and the closing date for the autumn lessons is the last day in July. Swimming lessons at Brockdale are very popular and numbers are limited. In order to secure a place for your child, please ensure that you apply as early as possible. We do have a waiting list for swimming classes, but people on it are more often than not disappointed.

Junior Gym

Our junior gym sessions are a great way for younger people to learn about the gym environment. Juniors between the ages of 12 and 15 can attend these sessions that are observed by our health and fitness team. In term times, the sessions are on Mondays, Wednesdays and Thursdays from 5 to 6 p.m. In holiday times, the sessions are on the same days, but from 2 - 3 p.m. Before a junior starts the sessions, he/she will need to complete an induction - please call the sports reception to book one.

Kids' Football

We all know that football is one of the most popular sports for both boys and girls. We run training sessions during term times and school holidays on Saturday mornings in the sports hall. The sessions start at 8 a.m. and go on until 1 p.m. (1 hour later in school holidays). The times and classes depend on the children's ages. These sessions are a lot of fun and are also very popular. Please call the sports reception for more information.

Children's Funky Dance

During the summer holidays, we offer our funky dance classes for seven weeks over the summer holidays. Kids from ages 8 to 14 can learn the funky moves to the latest songs in the charts.

Party! Party!

If you want to have a party for your child, then we have everything you need. Our party people will be delighted to organise and run your child's party and keep all the guests entertained with a range of games and sports activities. Our in-house catering department can discuss your food and drink requirements electronically or in person. Please note that the child celebrating the birthday must be aged five or above and does not need to be a member.

SECTION 2   Questions 15 – 27

Questions 15 – 21

Read the text on the following page and complete the sentences below.

Write NO MORE THAN THREE WORDS from the text for each answer.

Write your answers in boxes 15 - 21 on your answer sheet.

15   The _____ prices at the staff cafeteria always ensure that it's a dynamic place to meet other staff members and eat.

16   The _____ is the place to find the company gym.

17   Although employees can use the facilities, they have no _____ at the golf club.

18   Sponsoring the local football club helps develop awareness of the company within the town and _____ in consumers.

19   Travel to destinations for company social trips is usually done by _____.

20   The _____ was responsible for screening all childcare centres that accept the special childcare vouchers.

21   Employees don't need to worry about their _____, as the company has consulted with the Inland Revenue regarding staff benefits.

Company Benefits

Welcome to your new job with us and we hope you have a happy and long career. To help you enjoy life more and create a good work life balance, we provide various benefits for you.

Cafeteria

The staff cafeteria provides heavily subsidised meals for breakfast or lunch. The cafeteria opens weekdays from 6.30 a.m. and closes at 3 p.m. Reservations are never necessary. Because of the prices, the cafeteria is always a vibrant place to go, eat and socialise before work and in the middle of the working day.

Sport

We have our own gym in the annex next to our main building. If you'd like to use the gym, you need to undergo an induction session. Every other Monday, we have a fitness instructor who will come to our gym and give inductions to any staff who want to use the gym. Please do not use the gym without the induction. We also have a company membership at the town golf club. Our staff have playing and social membership access to the Club, but they do not have any voting rights in terms of how the Club is run and organised.

Watching Football

The company sponsors our local football club. This is a great method of expanding recognition of our company within the town and it can also help to influence customer brand loyalty. As a result of our sponsorship, we have a hospitality box at all home games and employees can take advantage of this for themselves and their families. There are 20 places available every week. If you want to book some places (limited to 3 per employee), please contact Andrew Hudson (ext. 734). If there are places available on the morning of the game, you can get more than 4 places.

Social Trips

The company runs periodical trips at weekends for staff. This might be to local places of interest, such as a castle or stately home, performances, such as theatre and classical or popular music, and museums, such as London's Tate Britain. We usually lay on a coach for transport and pay for the entry of the event. All trips will be advertised well in advance and places will be allocated on a 'first come, first served basis'. The trips are only for employees, but if there are places still available four days before the event, people may reserve places for friends and family. If the coach is not at least half booked by staff members four days before the event, the trip will be cancelled.

Childcare

We know that employees with children often have problems with organising quality childcare at affordable prices. Employees can take advantage of our special childcare vouchers that are redeemable at five childcare centres in town. All these centres have been screened and approved by our company management.

We have been in contact with the Inland Revenue Service and none of our staff benefits affects employees' annual tax liability.

Questions 22 – 27

Do the following statements agree with the information given in the text on the following page?

In boxes 22 – 27 on your answer sheet write:

TRUE	**if the statement agrees with the information**
FALSE	**if the statement contradicts the information**
NOT GIVEN	**if there is no information on this**

22   Working part-time is a possible form of flexible working.

23   Recent government legislation has made it compulsory for companies to consider employees' flexible working.

24   If employees have previously had a flexible working request turned down, they are not permitted to make another request.

25   The flexible working approval procedures were created in collaboration with the company's trade union representative.

26   Employees are required to give the reasons why they would like to change to flexible working.

27   Employees can have their flexible working request turned down if it will cause the company to spend more money.

Flexible Working in our Workplace

There are many forms of flexible working. It can describe a place of work, for example home-working, or a type of contract, such as a temporary contract. Other common variations include: part-time working, flexitime, job sharing and shift work.

Making a Request

Although employees with fewer than 26 weeks service do not have a statutory right to request flexible working, we allow all staff to make a request. To make a request for flexible working, employees must:

- make their request in writing, state the date the request is made, the change to working conditions they are seeking, and the date they would like the change to take effect
- state whether they have made a previous application for flexible work and the date of that application (this will not affect the new application)
- what change to working conditions they are seeking and how they think this may affect the business, e.g. cost saving to the business
- if they are making their request in relation to a health issue, e.g. as a reasonable adjustment for disabled employee.

How we Handle Requests to Work Flexibly

Once we have received a request, a manager will arrange a meeting as soon as possible with the employee to discuss it. This meeting can provide an opportunity to talk about what changes the employee is asking for and reasons for the change. Although the employee is not required to say why, this does allow compromises to be explored. The employee is allowed to be accompanied to a meeting by a work colleague or trade union representative.

Any request that is accepted will make a permanent change to the employment contract, so if the employee wants a temporary change, then any agreement will need to be put in writing.

We will consider all requests in a reasonable manner and we will only refuse them if there are business reasons for doing so. This reason must be from the following list:

- additional costs
- an inability to reorganise work amongst existing staff
- an inability to recruit additional staff
- a detrimental impact on quality
- a detrimental impact on performance
- a detrimental effect on ability to meet customer demand
- insufficient work for the periods the employee proposes to work
- planned structural changes to the business.

SECTION 3   Questions 28 – 40

Read the following text and answer Questions 28 – 40.

Paragraph A

Almost every summer, the amount of remaining Arctic ice gets smaller. The Arctic ice is vitally important to a whole range of animals from tiny shrimp and vast bowhead whales, and from polar bears to local people. By 2040, only a small amount of sea ice is projected to remain in the summer Arctic. Polar bears spend much of their time on the annual Arctic sea ice. It provides a platform for them to hunt, live, breed, and in some cases, create maternal dens.

Paragraph B

Polar bears are the top predator in the Arctic marine ecosystem. Because the polar bear's body requires a food selection based on large amounts of seal fat, they are the most carnivorous member of the bear family. However, food can be hard to come by for polar bears for much of the year. The bear puts on most of its yearly fat reserves between late April and mid-July to maintain its weight in the lean seasons. This food-free season can last three to four months, or even longer in areas like Canada's Hudson Bay. As the Arctic warms due to climate change, the ice pack is forming later in the season, and bears must wait longer to begin hunting again.

Paragraph C

Adult polar bears are solitary, but not anti-social; they actively seek mating partners in the late spring and early summer. Females begin to mate around the ages of four or five, but males take longer to mature and usually begin attempts to mate around the age of five or six, though their prime reproduction years begin around age ten. Males seek out females by following their scent, which means that two males often come across a female at the same time, leading to a potentially significant conflict. Polar bear couples are only together for about a week, and, after mating has taken place successfully, they go their separate ways.

Paragraph D

Today, the Arctic is warming roughly twice as fast as the global average, causing the ice that polar bears depend on to melt away. The sea ice is melting earlier and forming later each year. This makes it more difficult for females to get onto land in late autumn to den, and onto the sea ice in spring to feed. It means bears are fasting for longer, dramatically reducing their body weight and physical condition and making it harder for them to survive the summer season. Loss of sea ice is also a danger to the polar bear's main prey, seals, which depend on sea ice to raise their young and rest. Hunting has been a problem too, and recreational hunting has now been all but halted. Indigenous communities still have the right to hunt, as this is part of their culture, but this relatively small scale activity does not have a significant effect on bear numbers.

Paragraph E

In some regions, bears are spending more time on land. As sea ice decreases, the bears are spending more time on shore and the inquisitive and sometimes hungry bears enter towns and villages out of curiosity or to find food. Although community polar bear vigils keep curious, hungry bears away from town, they remain a problem every year, as until the ice returns, along

Paragraph F

It is important to identify critical ecosystems used by polar bears and other Arctic species. This includes key resting, feeding and birthing areas. These important areas need to receive special protection or management in order to safeguard the future for the people and wildlife that depend on the Arctic. One key area is protection from oil and gas exploration, which affects the delicate balance of the Arctic ecosystem. An oil spill not only harms polar bears, but also depletes their prey and contaminates their environment.

Paragraph G

In December last year, ministers and other national representatives from the five countries where polar bears are found - Canada, Norway, Denmark (Greenland), Russia and the United States - made commitments to help protect polar bears across their Arctic range. The declaration was made at the International Forum on Polar Bear Conservation in Russia, a forum that was also supported by the World Wide Fund for Nature. The declaration included commitments by the Arctic states to work on managing the polar bears' home in ways that will take into account the Arctic's shrinking ice and the increasing interest in Arctic development.

Paragraph H

One key way of helping polar bears is by monitoring them as they move around. Government researchers, in collaboration with the World Wide Fund for Nature, have set up a system that follows the bears' travels in the Arctic. Their positions are beamed from collars on the bears' necks, via satellite to scientists, and also to a specialised Internet site, so that the general public can become involved. This system allows the scientific group to get regular updates about how the polar bears behave in their Arctic environment and how they may be affected by climate change.

© The World Wide Fund for Nature

Questions 28 – 35

The text on the previous pages has 8 paragraphs (A – H).

Choose the correct heading for each section from the list of headings below.

Write the correct number (i – xi) in boxes 28 – 35 on your answer sheet.

i	International Collaboration
ii	Infertility Problems
iii	Breeding
iv	Significant Threats to Polar Bears
v	Tracking Bears
vi	Preserving Habitat
vii	Diet
viii	A Reduced Genetic Pool
ix	A Shrinking Habitat
x	Greater Funding Requirements
xi	Conflict with People

28   Paragraph A

29   Paragraph B

30   Paragraph C

31   Paragraph D

32   Paragraph E

33   Paragraph F

34   Paragraph G

35   Paragraph H

Questions 36 – 39

Do the following statements agree with the information given in the text?

In boxes 36 - 39 on your answer sheet write:

TRUE	**if the statement agrees with the information**
FALSE	**if the statement contradicts the information**
NOT GIVEN	**if there is no information on this**

36   Polar bears' feeding habits are fairly uniform throughout the year.

37   Towns affected by polar bear visits have set up their own patrols to help keep the bears away.

38   Zoos around the world are accelerating breeding programs to help build up polar bear numbers.

39   People around the world can take part in the monitoring of polar bear movements.

Question 40

Choose the correct letter, A, B, C or D.

Write the correct letter in box 40 on your answer sheet.

40   What is the best title for the text in Section 3?

A   The King of the Arctic
B   The Disappearing Land
C   A Threatened Breed
D   Climate Change in the North

GENERAL TRAINING WRITING PRACTICE TEST

TASK 1

You should spend about 20 minutes on this task.

You have an interview next week for a job you really want, but unfortunately you will now be unable to attend.

Write a letter to the person due to interview you. In your letter,

- **inform him and apologise**
- **explain the reason why you cannot come to the interview**
- **offer a new day and time and express your continued desire for the job**

You should write at least 150 words.

*You do **NOT** need to write any addresses. Begin your letter as follows:*

Dear Mr. Compton,

TASK 2

You should spend about 40 minutes on this task.

People today often have children at a later age than they used to. What do you feel are the reasons for this? Is it a positive or negative phenomenon?

You should write at least 250 words.

GENERAL TRAINING SPEAKING PRACTICE TEST

Section 1

- Can you describe the city/town/village where you live?
- Is this a good place to live?
- Would you prefer to live in a city or in the countryside? (Why?)

Topic 1   Smoking

- Do you smoke? (Why/Why not?)
- At what age do you think smoking should be legal?
- Do you think that smoking should be banned from all indoor places, as has already happened in some countries?
- How can governments stop people from smoking?

Topic 2   Social Media

- Why do you think social media is so popular nowadays?
- How do you think social media will change over the next 10 years?
- What are some of the dangers that social media can represent?
- How can we reduce the fascination that young people have with social media, or shouldn't we be worried?

Section 2

> Describe a memorable journey that you once took
>   You should say:
>   where this journey was
>   when this journey was
>   what you did during the journey
>   and explain why this journey is so memorable for you.

Section 3

Topic 1   Travel

- Why do you think people enjoy travel?
- What can people learn from travel?
- How has travel changed over the last 50 years?
- What are some of the negative impacts of so much travel nowadays?

Topic 2   Air Travel

- What are some of the dangers of air travel?
- What are some of the reasons that budget air travel has increased so much in popularity recently?
- How do you feel air travel will change over the next 30 years?
- Should governments restrict the amount of air travel nowadays and how could they do this?

GENERAL TRAINING PRACTICE TEST ANSWERS

LISTENING TEST ANSWERS				READING TEST ANSWERS			
1	Carol	21	seminars	1	C	21	(annual) tax liability
2	34	22	accents	2	A	22	TRUE
3	HT8 5RD	23	children	3	E	23	NOT GIVEN
4	Credit card	24	names	4	D	24	FALSE
5	Economy (size)	25	marketing	5	B	25	NOT GIVEN
6	(An) emergency pack	26	(language) variation	6	C	26	FALSE
7	45 litres	27	supervisor	7	D	27	TRUE
8	(At) (the) airport	28	deadlines	8	E	28	ix
9	(A) (basic) map	29	survey	9	A	29	vii
10	(About) a mile	30	statistics	10	B	30	iii
11	4	31	freshwater	11	C	31	iv
12	(management) committee	32	critical list	12	A	32	xi
13	volunteers	33	(fierce) appearance	13	C	33	vi
14	(local) government (area)	34	identification	14	D	34	i
15	staff	35	breeding cycle	15	(heavily) subsidised	35	v
16	matches	36	habitat	16	annex	36	FALSE
17	musicians	37	hole size	17	(voting) rights	37	TRUE
18	dance	38	(endangered) species	18	(brand) loyalty	38	NOT GIVEN
19	(local) police	39	(Heavy) chain	19	coach	39	TRUE
20	maps	40	(A) (marker) float	20	(company) management	40	C

/ indicates an alternative answer
( ) indicates an optional part of answer

Note: The Listening Test transcript showing answers' locations in sentences can be downloaded on our website: visit http://www.ielts-blog.com/book-practice-test/

WRITING TEST MODEL RESPONSES

TASK 1

Dear Mr. Compton,

I am writing regarding my interview with you next week on Thursday morning. I am very sorry to say that I will not be able to come to the interview, because my cousin is having an operation.

My cousin and I are very close and she has asked me specifically to be with her before and after the procedure. Unfortunately, the operation date was only set yesterday morning and I therefore was unable to predict that I would not be able to meet you on Thursday.

I am very disappointed not to be able to attend, as your company and the position interest me greatly. I sincerely hope that you might be able to offer me an alternative day for the interview. I can come at any time before or after next Thursday and I can fit in with what I expect is your busy schedule.

Thank you for your consideration and I am looking forward to hearing from you.

Yours sincerely,
Julia Broad

TASK 2

Over the last one hundred years, there has been a definite trend for people to have children later in life than they used to. It cannot be clearly proved why this has come about and there are certain advantages and disadvantages to this situation.

One reason why people have children later is related to some basic changes in society. Relationships between people in the past were often on a much more formal basis. The process of setting up a family was generally started much earlier, as early marriage was the main way of a man and a woman starting a relationship. Today, especially in the west, people often live with each other before getting married and so there is less inclination to begin the process of having children. In addition, the fact that women are now equally active in their jobs has led many of them to desire to exploit their career potential while they are younger rather than having a life caring for children.

This situation has various advantages. Firstly, the society changes that have allowed women more choice in their lives, so that they can enjoy the challenges of a career, have led to improved gender equality. Two people having children later in life also means that they will probably be more affluent and therefore better able to provide a financially secure environment for a child to grow up in.

Naturally, there are also disadvantages. Having children later in life creates more risks for the woman and for the baby. Fortunately, modern advances in medicine can cope with many of these challenges. In terms of the family dynamic, as bringing up a child is an exhausting process, families started later can make older parents suffer more pressure, as they have less resilience. Older parents also have less chance of enjoying the benefits of seeing grandchildren and great grandchildren.

In conclusion, changes in society dynamics seem to be responsible for why people today often start families later in life. There are mixed positive and negative aspects to this and the choice for parents regarding starting a family should be made with these in mind.

SPEAKING SAMPLE PRACTICE TEST – Examiner's Commentary

Please download the Speaking Sample Practice test recording and transcript on the following web page: http://www.ielts-blog.com/book-practice-test/

Below is the Examiner's Commentary on Katrin's performance in the recorded Speaking test, including her estimated IELTS Band Score.

<u>Examiner's Commentary</u>

The person interviewed is Katrin, a German female. Katrin is an office administrator.

<u>Section 1</u>

Katrin spoke fluently and accurately. She did not need to pause for language and gave full answers. She had a good vocabulary range, though she used the occasional awkward choice ("metropole" and "to their side" instead of 'at their sides'). There were very few grammar errors. Katrin had an accent, but a it was often negligible.

<u>Section 2</u>

Katrin spoke fluently for the allocated time. Her pronunciation was again very good, though she showed an error with pronouncing the 'v' in ("visited" and "individual"), which is not uncommon for Germans. There were a few minor grammar and word choice errors ("the first time I did that" instead of 'I had done that' + "everyone had its own character" instead of 'their own character' + 'did a journey' instead of 'made a journey'). None of the errors created any problems with comprehension.

<u>Section 3</u>

Again, Katrin showed her good ability at English. Her vocabulary choices were good, her grammar mostly accurate and her pronunciation clear. Pauses were only to consider her replies. She showed a sense of humour, which is always a nice thing to do, as it creates a relaxed atmosphere, where people can perform more effectively.

Marking - The marking of the IELTS Speaking Test is done in 4 parts.

<u>Fluency and Coherence</u>	7
<u>Lexical Resource</u>	7
<u>Grammatical Range and Accuracy</u>	7
<u>Pronunciation</u>	8
Estimated IELTS Speaking Band	**7**

49693572R00051

Made in the USA
Middletown, DE
23 October 2017